2—

WISDOM
From the Corner

INSPIRATIONAL STORIES BUILDING CHAMPIONS IN LIFE

BY
JOSÉ CAMPO

Tate Publishing, LLC

DEDICATION

I want to dedicate this book to my parents, Joe and Betsy Campo. They were the perfect teammates during their 48 years of marriage. It is said that the highest form of flattery is to imitate someone. I loved my dad so much that I wanted to be just like him. He was a role model of high moral standards and dedication to our family and the athletes he coached. On the outside, he was as tough as they come, but on the inside, his heart was always soft. Even though my Mom is in heaven, I know she is proud of me and approves of the things I am trying to do. She was the perfect mother, grandmother and mother-in-law. I miss my Mom and look forward to the day we meet in paradise.

To my wife Stacey, I dedicate my life. You are and always will be the MVP of our family.

To my daughters Serena and Toya ~ the greatest gift God could ever give me is you.

ACKNOWLEDGEMENTS

I want to express my appreciation to the following individuals who inspire, support and believe in me–I am a blessed man to have your friendship.

Ryan Tate ~ without your encouragement and belief in me, I would have never taken the chance to step out and write this book.

Bobby Antonacci ~ a true friend is one who cares enough to tell you when you are screwing up. Thanks Bobby!

Jerry Goodfellow ~ you are my best friend and closer than any brother I have. Thank you for always being there for me. I love you.

Miles McPherson ~ my pastor at the Rock. For the last fifteen years, you have led me spiritually and given me the push to always obey God. My family is blessed to have a pastor like you.

Donnie Dee, Derrick Roth, and the staff of FCA ~ your love of God and high school athletes has always been an inspiration to me. Whenever I felt down, you always reminded me that coaches are the most influential people in America.

Scott Glabb ~ thanks for always believing in my ability to touch high school wrestlers.

Gail Miller, Joe Tezak and all of our Mt. Carmel wrestling family ~ you are my sons, my friends and my biggest fans. Thank you for all of the hard work and dedication over the years. You are the reason I coach.

Tom, Glen, Gary, Mark and Patsy ~ working with you at Mt. Carmel has been rewarding and fun. Your dedication and love for kids, encourages me to come to work everyday. Thanks for being my friends.

~ José

FOREWORD

As a staff person with the Fellowship of Christian Athletes I have had the privilege to develop friendships with many athletes, coaches, donors, staff and volunteers. It has been said that coaches are the most influential people in America. I believe this to be true because of the influence a few coaches had on my life and because of the role I see coaches playing in the lives of young people everyday.

What a blessing to watch God use Coach Campo to help shape and direct young athletes both physically and spiritually. Whether it's the Bible study he leads at Mt Carmel High School or the 60 wrestlers for Christ he challenges at FCA camp, there have been hundreds of lives that will never be the same because of the way this coach lives his life.

Wisdom from the Corner is a book about some of those young athletes and their stories. You will be inspired as you read about their struggles and their accomplishments. You will also be encouraged in your own walk with Christ as you learn from Coach's spiritual journey.

This book is full of many life principles that will bless any parent, businessmen, coach or athlete. Coach Campo was influenced most by his dad, the Gov. They say "a father shapes the son and the son reflects the father." This is certainly true and you will see the beauty of this statement in the pages of this book.

"But none of these things move me, nor do I count my life dear to myself, that I might finish my race with joy and the ministry that I have received from the Lord Jesus, to testify of the Gospel of the Grace of God." Acts 20:24.

Coach Campo reminds me of this verse. He has run the race well. He has honored the Lord in his family life, teaching life and coaching life. Coach Campo is an example to us all. I thank God for you, Coach!!

Teammates in Christ,
Donnie Dee, Regional Director
Fellowship of Christian Athletes

CONTENTS

PART ONE: MY TESTIMONY

PART TWO: KEYS TO SUCCESS

PART THREE: A BLESSED LIFE

PART ONE
My Testimony

Chapter One

BORN TO COACH
Son of the 'Gov'

After coaching for 28 years, I have learned that kids have many choices in their lives to make. But the one choice they don't have is the parents they are born to. I want everyone to know that I was blessed to be born to coach.

My dad was the greatest high school wrestling and football coach in the history of New York State. He is known in the wrestling fraternity as the "Governor of Wrestling", or as we call him, "The Gov". Whether it was football, wrestling or baseball season, I wanted to spend all my time with the Gov. During those years; I had so many of his athletes tell me that my dad was the most important, most influential person in their lives. That made such an impact on me that I would say to myself, *wouldn't that be nice if someday, someone could say that about me?* Because of past experiences like those mentioned I knew at a very young age all I wanted to do was to be like my dad. I tried to walk like him, talk like him, sign my name like him and even comb my hair like him. I wanted to be a teacher and coach, even someday be called 'Coach Campo', just like my dad.

At the early age of 3, I used to put on wrestling demonstrations with my brother, Mike, before the high school matches. At four years old, my Mom would give me the Gov's lunch and I would walk three blocks (by myself) up to his high school to eat with him. I would then spend the rest of the day with my dad in his Physical Education classes, watching and listening to every move he made and observing him as he coached. Because of this, I became a sports addict, knowing the rules and techniques of every sport imaginable. I was a stud athlete at the very early age of five—because everything in my life revolved around sports.

One day while I was playing outside our apartment, a young man drove up in a beautiful brand new sports car. It was a 1964 Corvette Convertible and I had never seen anything like it before. I ran over to his car and asked him where he got it.

He told me, "If you graduate from West Point, they give you one."

The man's name was Freddie Grates and he was the first wrestler my dad ever sent to West Point. Freddie walked to our door with this huge yearbook in his hand. On the cover was an inscription saying, *"Thanks for everything, Coach. I couldn't have done it without you."* I saw a look of pride on the Gov's face that I will never forget. I lived the rest my life trying to put that same look on my dad's face. In everything I ever did, all I wanted to hear from my dad was, "I am proud of you, Son."

I started wrestling on the freshman level when I was in fourth grade. My family lived in a very small town in upstate New York called Frankfort. As the football and wrestling coach, my dad was the "king" of the town. He turned the local high school in this little Italian town into an athletic powerhouse. Even today, he has former athletes who are now fifty to sixty years old, who call him up and thank him for the role he played in their lives. Ever since the Gov left that town, it has been like a ghost town with only memories of the victories and the glory from the late 50s and early 60s.

Dad always wanted a better environment and more opportunities for his wife and six children. When we lived in upstate New York, our house was actually a one-bedroom apartment. Imagine living with six children in such a small place. We didn't even have a bathroom. All we had was a toilet, sticking out of my parent's bedroom wall. In order to take a bath, we had to go upstairs to the landlord's apartment to use her tub.

Financially, it was very difficult, raising six children on a teacher's salary. Even though we had very little in the way of material possessions, my Mom made us feel like we had everything we ever wanted. Friday nights were "party time" at the Campo home. Watching TV with soda and chips, the Campo kids were *in heaven.*

The people of Frankfort loved the Gov. On Friday nights before the football games, high school students would start a pep rally outside our apartment and sing the school's fight song. They would call for my Dad to come out and give a pep talk. The championship football and wrestling teams the Gov coached had this town busting with pride. Therefore, you can understand why I was so confused when my Dad told our family that we were moving to Long Island.

The Gov took over as football and wrestling coach at Brentwood High School on eastern Long Island. He went ahead of our family to find us a home and start football practice. It was a long three months for my Mom, handling 6 children on her own before we could join the Gov.

In Brentwood, I was introduced to organized athletics when my Dad signed me up for Little League Baseball and Pop Warner Football. The coaches were impressed with my abilities and I became one of the stars of the team at 11 years of age, scoring touchdowns and hitting homeruns. Therefore, I began to get recognition as a young boy and affirmation that I was a very good athlete. Of course, now I understand it was because of the hours spent practicing along side the older boys during the Gov's high school practices. **Hard work** would be the first ingredient of my formula for a blessed life.

As I got older, I found out that the pressure of being the coach's son was overwhelming. In wrestling, I was not only supposed to win, but I was supposed to dominate my opponents. It was very difficult to wrestle under that kind of stress and I'll never forget my first match as a seventh grader. Right before the match started, the gym doors open up and the Gov walks in with the whole Varsity wrestling team, to watch me. It was my first match and I was so nervous. I was taken down and pinned in front of my Dad and that was very, very hard to accept because I did not see that look of pride that I so wanted.

One of the main reasons my Dad's teams were so successful was that he coached expecting absolute perfection. Anything less was unacceptable in the Gov's book. After dinner on many occasions, he would sit me down and tell me all the different things I did wrong in practice. Reviewing the videotapes after a match or football game, the Gov would call me up to the table and show me all the mistakes I had made. He seemed to go on and on—it was very hard to please my Dad. Where was that look of pride?

Chapter 2

WHO ARE YOU TRYING TO PLEASE?
Through High School

In my ninth-grade year, the other kids had finally caught up with me athletically. Instead of following the examples of all my Dad's great champions, by working hard and doing the right things, I started looking for shortcuts.

The number one challenge of most wrestlers, including myself is weight control. Although you always wrestle someone your own size, if you are two ounces over the weight class limit, you don't wrestle! Trying to control the amount of food you eat or liquid you drink, especially around Thanksgiving and Christmas is very tough! This is what sets the sport of wrestling apart from all other sports. Instead of eating nutritious foods and exercising hard, I looked for new weight-control method. The one method I found to be very successful allowed me to eat as much food as I wanted and not gain an ounce! Today, this method is known as "bulimia", a word that was unheard of when I was a young wrestler.

My older brother introduced me to this new method. You ate what you wanted, but then puked it all back up shortly after. One night, he took me into our bathroom and started taking off his belt. He began swallowing one end of it to make himself vomit. I started using this method and was amazed at how successful I was at controlling my weight. To make sure my parents didn't hear me, I would wake up at 3 o'clock in the morning and head to the refrigerator. I would eat as much food as I could, then walk to my bathroom and barf up everything I had just eaten. I was looking for short cuts without thinking about what consequences the future might bring. I would vomit until I could taste the acid coming from my stomach. Little did I know, the hydrochloric acid which helps digest your food could actually eat through metal. I also didn't realize that the destruction of the enamel on my teeth, which was caused by this acid, was permanent. Today, I continue to pay for those decisions, with my constant visits to the dentist office.

My second shortcut method came in a different form. Saturday nights were unique, because I wouldn't vomit. I would take laxatives. The Ex-Lax box would say to take 1–2 pills to relieve constipation—I would take 8 of them! Before going to bed, I would clear out a path to the bathroom and then spending my entire Sunday on the toilet.

I later learned that through vomiting and taking laxatives, the body loses important electrolytes. These electrolytes help the heart beat at a normal rhythm. With the intense wrestling I was doing, I could have easily died from what I was putting my body through. With a routine of daily vomiting, I eventually ruptured my esophagus and had to be rushed to the hospital. Due to my lifestyle choices, I was unable to wrestle my entire junior year of high school. Today, I continue to pay for my shortcuts. I can't go any where after eating without a bathroom nearby. Certain foods eaten prohibit me from controlling my bowel movements.

This is one area I feel kids are missing today—there are consequences for every decision made. They don't think that their choices have consequences and how those consequences may affect their lives forever.

The Gov was a recruiter for West Point. He thought that the education and athletic programs at the United States Military Academy were second to none. His belief was that a West Point graduate would never have a problem getting a good job. All this, plus, tuition, room and board was free! The fact that West Point was only two hours from our house also didn't hurt. Dad believed that anybody who could qualify to go to school at West Point should go. So there was no doubt as to where Mike, my older brother and hero, was going to college. At this time I was entering the 10th grade. Everyone in my high school expected me to follow in the same athletic steps of my brother. Mike was a great three-sport athlete and since we played the same three sports, it made sense that I too, would achieve greatness.

Some people are blessed with athletic ability, but Mike was a great athlete because of the amount of hard work he put into his sports. Being the first child, the Gov pushed my older brother harder than any other athlete. He would make Mike run long distances on Sundays with ankle weights on. He was the champion of our family. If you ask me about my greatest sports memories, it would have to involve something Mike achieved. Whether it was being a county wrestling champion as a sophomore, or scoring four goals in lacrosse against Navy. Mike was my hero. I was president of his fan club and also Mike's loudest cheerleader. My grandparents couldn't sit next to me while Mike was wrestling, because of how loud I would scream for him. A star in three sports, Mike won the Outstanding Athlete award for our high school. I can remember seeing Dad cry when Mike won the award.

Once again, I saw that look of pride on Dad's face. I wanted to please the Gov and was lucky enough to have the perfect example of how to do it, sleeping in the bunk bed right above me. If something was good enough for my brother, it was surely good enough for me. So when Mike said, "Stick this belt down your throat," I didn't ask, "why." More about that later.

As hard as I tried, I could never equal the success my brother achieved. I was blessed with athletic ability, but I didn't work nearly as hard as Mike. My goal was to be as successful as Mike, but I seemed to fall short of that goal every time I stepped out on the mat. Instead of winning the tournaments, I always took second. You could easily pick me out of the pictures on the awards stand. I was always the one with his head down. My head was down because 2nd place was not good enough, especially for Joe Campo's son. The high school teams Dad coached were different from most high schools. You see, we were always number #1—the winners; **never** second place.

From 7th grade to when I graduated high school, the Gov's teams never lost a match or tournament. In football, he only lost one game in that same time span. So, my *second* place finishes were hard on Dad. My self image and my dad's image of me was always one of disappointment.

Even though I strived to be a champion, the lifestyle choices I was making didn't reflect that desire. At this point in my life, although I was ashamed of my past behaviors and the dangerous methods of weight control, I still continued to use them. My weight at the start of wrestling season was 115 pounds. Our team was so tough, the only way I could make the starting lineup was to lose 17 pounds and wrestle 98. I can remember thinking about how much my parents sacrificed to put food on the table for six children. In short, I was taking that same food and just flushing it down the toilet every time I forced myself to throw-up. This knowledge, however, did not stop me.

I knew just what foods I could eat that would come back up easily. My best friend, Jerry Goodfellow knew all the fast food restaurants, which had locking bathroom doors. We would go to McDonalds and drink three milkshakes each. Then, one at a time, we would go into the bathroom and puke up all the milkshakes. There was momentary satisfaction in being able to taste the forbidden food and still work towards my goal and ultimate desire to please Dad.

As mentioned previously, when you take shortcuts, there are always consequences. Sometimes those consequences are more life altering than others. I remember the day when my shortcuts put me in the hospital with a ruptured esophagus. I had finished practice and stopped at the store to buy a quart of apple juice. I guzzled it down and immediately puked it back up, using the empty bottle to collect my vomit. I knew I wouldn't gain any weight if I could fill the bottle back up.

At this point in my bulimia sickness, I no longer needed anything to help stimulate my body to vomit. All I had to do was shake my body around and get the food in my stomach moving and up it came! This particular night, my throat started hurting and my parents rushed me to the hospital. I lied and said I had been hit in the throat during practice. The doctors discovered my ruptured esophagus. After spending a week in the hospital, I was able to go home.

However, my return home was short lived as I returned to the hospital a couple days later to have my appendix taken out. The doctors would not allow me to finish the wrestling season. I felt, at the time, it was the doctor's fault or decision to end my season early; *it had nothing to do with my shortcuts.* In my youthful mind, I felt it was not my fault that my body gave out and I was just thankful that at least I could eat!

My senior year came and the old patterns continued. I never accepted responsibility for my lifestyle choices nor was I a champion. Losing to wrestlers that had no business beating me became common. I had played the same three sports in high school as my brother, but never came close to his accomplishments. On the other hand, when people would ask the Gov how Mike was doing at West Point, he would get a smile on his face; that smile of pride.

Since I couldn't please my Dad athletically, I thought to myself, *maybe if I went to West Point, Dad would be proud of me, too.* Even though I wanted to become a high school teacher and coach, like the Gov, I felt my going to West Point would make him proud and happy, for once.

Chapter 3

DECISIONS WE MAKE TO PLEASE OTHERS, USUALLY RESULT IN CONFLICT AND DISASTER
West Point Years

My brother was a senior at West Point when I entered as a freshman and was more fondly referred to as a "plebe." I'll never forget my very first day there. Following dinner, I was marching back to my room by myself when I noticed two cadets standing in the courtyard watching me. As I got closer I saw it was my brother Mike and the captain of the basketball team, Pete Jackson. When they saw me marching so seriously, they cracked up laughing.

They yelled, "Hey Campo, get over here."

The closer I got to them, the more they laughed. My brother Mike was voted captain of the wrestling team, a very prestigious position. The one thing he had in common with Pete Jackson was that they both hated West Point.

Pete said to me, "So, how do you like this place?"

I responded, "This place sucks!"

That made Mike and Pete laugh even harder.

Pete came up with an idea he thought would be funny. The very next morning, when I was standing in formation, he came up from behind and started talking to me. Pete used this mean voice and I didn't know who it was.

Pete said, "Hey Campo, every time you hear me say, 'Hey, Campo,' you have to yell out, 'I love it here, Sir.' You got that?"

So every morning, whenever Pete would wake up, he would open the window from his bedroom and yell out, "Hey, Campo."

Then I would have to scream, "I love it here, Sir."

Since I was lying, I could have been thrown out of West Point for breaking their honor code of not lying, cheating or stealing or tolerating anyone who did. I really hated it at West Point. As a senior, my brother Mike had many privileges at West Point, compared to a plebe. Of course, I wanted to hang around my brother all the time.

That spring break, all the cadets were able to go home—except for us freshmen. I was with some hockey players and they asked me if I wanted to "go party."

I thought they just wanted to drink some beers. So, ignoring the fact that drinking was not allowed at West Point, I said, "Sure, I'll go with you."

We walked through the woods for about fifteen minutes until we came to their secret partying place where they had some warm beers to drink. We sat down and started drinking, when one of the hockey players took out some marijuana. In high school, I was a pretty straight guy. I drank beer before, but had not yet acquired a taste for it. But smoking pot was for *druggies* and I was not one of them. They lit up the joint and start passing it around. They passed it to me and there came the test of my courage and beliefs. I wanted to be "cool" and considered one of their friends. I didn't have the courage to say no, so I grabbed it and started smoking. You *hear* about peer pressure and there I was, suddenly a victim of it. Little did I know, this would start a drug problem that would last ten years. Can you imagine? I am at this prestigious college, known for its discipline. I hate it there and now I am drinking beer and smoking pot. I went to West Point to please my Dad and compete in athletics. I am not sure when I lost complete sight of my goal.

The summer before my sophomore year at West Point was spent learning how to be an Army officer. We spent our time doing Army things like marching and drilling. We were at a camp near West Point and it was there that I met other class-mates who were also athletes. Since they lived far away, I would take them to my home for any weekends we had free. We led the same type of lifestyle that included drugs and alcohol, not ever concerned about consequences. My brother had graduated and once again, I had an opportunity hopefully to make my family proud of me.

However, my goal did not go as planned. My second year at West Point was worse than the first. I had a second major sur-gery that ended all chances of wrestling. Against doctor's orders, I tried out for the lacrosse team. The coach knew about my ques-tionable lifestyle and didn't want to put up with an undisciplined team member. My brother could step off the wrestling mat one-day, pick up his lacrosse stick and score 4 goals. When I did not show the same athletic ability, cutting me from the team was easy for the coach. When I did not make the lacrosse team, I rationalized that it was okay, because I would have more time to party.

That was about the time I started learning how to get answers on upcoming tests from other cadets at West Point. A shortcut that made it possible for me to not study, and be able to sneak out every night into the woods and get high. Can you imagine? I originally went to West Point to compete in athletics, graduate and make my family proud. By now my life consisted of using drugs and cheating on every test I took. Not exactly what West Point stood for or what I had planned.

Even though there is no tuition cost at West Point, you owe a five-year military obligation to the Army upon gradua-tion. West Point is different then your typical 4-year college in that you had no choice in the classes you took because everyone had the same major. We took 18 credits a semester, and went to classes six days a week. Everyone at West Point would graduate with a General Engineering degree. We did get to choose from the few electives and I would choose the easiest ones. After my sophomore year, I had all my general education requirements out of the way. I will never forget when an academic counselor looked at my class selection and told me there was no rhyme or reason for the classes I was taking. They weren't pointing in any direction.

The counselor asked about my choices, "What do you want to do after you graduate?"

I told the counselor that I wanted to be a high school teacher and coach, just like my Dad. Right then the officer looked at me and said, "You are at the wrong school, son."

Under my breath I said to myself, *just tell my Dad that!*

I could have easily transferred from West Point after the first two years and gone to any college I wanted. But the word "quit" was unacceptable and never used in our family. There was no quitting.

It was my sophomore year, when I got in serious trouble for the first time. I had to write an English paper, so I asked my roommate if he had any papers that I could use. He had English the first semester, so I decided to use one of his. I rewrote the paper and turned it in. When the rest of the class got their graded papers back, I got a note saying, "Your paper is being looked at for documentary deficiencies." I didn't know what that meant.

I went back to my room and talked to my roommate. I asked if there was anything I should know about the paper that he gave me?

Kenny said, "No, there's nothing wrong with it."

Little did I know, my roommate had used Cliff Notes to write the paper. In fact, he took 99% of the paper all from Cliff Notes. I had a different instructor than Kenny and just my luck, mine taught directly from Cliff Notes. The English Department had me dead! They were ready to kick me out for plagiarism.

At West Point, when you're brought up on cheating or "honor charges", they take you to court and use cadets on the jury. They listen to the case and decide whether you're guilty or not. If you're found guilty, you get kicked out of West Point. Luckily for me, I knew one of the jurors. He was a person on the wrestling team, and came to me saying, "If you can make up a story that is any way believable, I'll vote you not guilty."

So I made up some kind of story and was found 'not guilty'. Instead of just getting off "scot-free", I was given a six-month penalty of room confinement. For six months, I couldn't leave my room except for going to my classes. I couldn't go to any football games, except for the Army-Navy game. I did not want to come back for my junior year. West Point's rules state that if you leave or get kicked out within your first two years, there is no military obligation. Once you start your junior year and quit or get kicked out, you owe a four-year obligation in the army as a private. Knowing that my Dad would never allow me to quit, I headed back for my junior year.

In 1976, my Junior year at West Point, my life changed—for the worse. I was involved in the largest cheating scandal in the history of West Point. I was given a take-home test that everyone in the whole junior class (about one thousand kids) was given. It was ten pages long, worth about 1% of your final grade, and due in a week.

Of course I went to my friends, some of the smarter guys there, and got help. They gave me all the answers I needed and headed back to my room. My roommate, another kid taking shortcuts like me, looked at my paper, copied all the answers down and we turned it in.

Now as juniors, we were allowed to leave West Point during spring break. After we turned in our ten-page test, one of the cadets wrote down on the bottom of a sheet of paper that he had gotten help from another cadet. He was basically turning himself in, admitting that he cheated on the test. The result of that confession was the start of the largest cheating scandal that West Point had ever seen.

The 1976 cheating scandal was in the newspapers and on all TV stations around the country. Any time something goes wrong at one of the military academies, it makes national news. Over two hundred kids were brought up for cheating.

In my first trial, I had another friend on the jury and was found 'not guilty'. Fifty other cadets were not so lucky. These fifty cadets knew that cheating was more widespread at West Point and now had to make it public knowledge. The Academy also knew that more cadets were involved. The strategy of the fifty found guilty was to make this scandal so big that there would be no way West Point would throw out 200 to 300 cadets. Those fifty came up with the names of over 300 other cadets they knew cheated. In the end over 150 cadets were eventually found guilty and kicked out. When the officials of West Point looked at this scandal, they knew many people were to blame. West Point conducted a thorough investigation after the scandal. They came to the conclusion that changes had to be made within the system, to encourage working together, but not cheating on tests.

In the spring of 1976, I was brought up on charges for violation of the Code of Honor, (simply put. . . . cheating). I was to stand before a jury of Army officers who would decide my future at West Point. Their decision was made in early July of 1976 and I was found guilty. I was asked to leave along with 151 other young men.

The hardest part of all of this experience had yet to be played out. My next move was to call the Gov and tell him the reason I had to come home. When I made that phone call, he didn't understand me and kept asking, "Why?"

"Dad, I just got kicked out of West Point for cheating."

There was silence on the other end of the line.

Thank God for my mother who was on the other line.

She told me she "still loved me and to come home—everything is going to be okay."

My Dad didn't say a word.

If it had not been for Mom saying those words, I probably would have wanted to kill myself. Although I was not the only boy going home in shame, but, it did not make the trip any easier. I was still going home as the West Point cheater.

When people would ask the Gov, "How's your son doing at West Point?" my Dad wouldn't pull any punches.

He would tell everyone right away, "He got kicked out for cheating."

I spent the next four months at my parents' house. I started coaching at my old high school. I coached the J.V. football team and helped the Gov with his wrestling team. The sad part was my lifestyle choices were still the same. I continued smoking pot and drinking beer, even though it was driving my father and me farther and father apart.

Since so many cadets were involved in the scandal and asked to leave West Point, the publicity had a very negative impact on the school. As a result, West Point began to realize how the procedure of a take home test given to the 1000 cadets could only result in some form of cheating. Therefore in the fall of 1976, West Point resended their decision and gave all 152 expelled cadets an option to return. We could take a year off and then return to finish our senior year and graduate. This would include completing the 5-year obligation of service due after graduation.

The Gov thought this was a great idea. Here was my chance to go back and graduate, but I also had the chance of leaving West Point without any kind of military obligation. In an effort to persuade me, the Gov had all different people come and talk to me including some of his closest friends. I'll never forget an assistant principal meeting the Gov at the door of our house and telling him, "Don't worry, Joe, I'll talk him into it."

My old J.V football coach, an ex-military man, sat me

down at our kitchen table trying to tell me how I needed to go back and finish my senior year at West Point. Of course, I got mad at him and started yelling and screaming.

"You don't know what the heck you're talking about. You didn't go to West Point, so how can you tell me what it's all about?"

My old coach yelled back at me, trying to get me to sit down. I walked out of the house, furious at my Dad and my coach.

That night, my older brother, Mike, called. He had graduated from West Point and was already an officer in the Army. I told him everything that was going on and he told me, "Listen, don't worry about what Mom and Dad say. It's your life. The Army sucks. You can go and transfer to another college."

That's all I needed to hear to form my decision. I would not be returning to West Point. Instead, I would seek out another university to finish my undergrad education. West Point did everything in their power to convince us to stay. This included telling us that we were going to be "labeled as failures." In many ways, I already had accepted that label.

The West Point people told us, "No other college would let us transfer to their college, once you have been kicked out of West Point—everyone is going to know that you're a cheater and that you got kicked out—no college will want you."

Chapter 4

HOW YOUR LIFE CAN INFLUENCE OTHERS
Party Life 1976–84

It was time for me to start looking for another college. I needed to get out of the house and finish my education. I remember going to visit colleges in the area. After three years at West Point, I left with 120 credits in general engineering. Usually it takes about 126 credits to graduate from a normal college. With 120 already under my belt, you would think I didn't have many hours left to complete with as degree.

Instead of trying to graduate as fast as possible, I decided that it was time for me to stop trying to please everyone and please myself. I had always wanted to be a high school Physical Education teacher, therefore that was what I was going to do. I looked around at different colleges and finally heard about this small college in New Haven, Connecticut. Southern Connecticut State College was a Division II school and the wrestling coach there was, Don Knauf.

Coach Knauf knew my Dad and also knew that my body was torn up. I wasn't going to be able to compete and Coach Knauf was nice enough to offer me a non-paying coaching position on his staff. He was the first one to make me feel wanted by telling me how helpful I would be just being in the wrestling room. Those statements were the first bit of good news I had heard from anybody in a long time. So I found myself attending Southern.

I started in the second semester, right after Christmas. I drove up to New Haven and moved in with a bunch of wrestlers. Of course, part of my plan to please myself was to do whatever I wanted and that meant putting some serious time into living the college party life. As a student at Southern Connecticut, I was ready to make up for the time that I missed by going to West Point for three long years.

I fit right in with the wrestlers, especially with my beautiful stereo that I brought from West Point. On my first night on campus, I had the seven other wrestlers, who were living in the house, in my bedroom and we were set to party. We were getting high and listening to rock music, really loud when my bedroom door opens up and there stood the head coach and his little son. Of course, like dumb kids, we thought we could hide from the coach if we just turned off the lights. Lucky for me, Coach Knauf didn't say anything about that night. I am very appreciative to Coach Knauf and the opportunity he gave me. He could have ended my coaching career even before it started.

Southern not only gave me an opportunity to finish my degree, but it also gave me my start into the coaching arena and to begin to develop my skills. At West Point, I was continually told what a poor leader I was, however, my mom had believed in my ability and me, my entire life, even at an early age. She would encourage me by saying that I was a natural leader, and despite what I had done up to that point with my talents, she never lost faith.

God Has a Plan for your life— whether you agree or not

At Southern Connecticut, I was given the opportunity to conduct all the wrestling practices. Coach Knauf was a great recruiter, but I knew a lot more about wrestling. I had learned from many great coaches and I was confident of my abilities.

This was an opportunity to make my own mark and do things differently than my Dad. One of my major differences was to try to make things fun. Wrestling is a tough sport and practices are hard work. I learned I could get more out of the wrestlers if I made practices fun. That year our team had 28 wins, which was the third most wins of any college team in the United States. We qualified 7 wrestlers to the Nationals, but life has a way of always making bad decisions have consequences. Coach Knauf did not reward my successes, (maybe he remembered that first night on campus), I am not sure, but he did not ask me to accompany him and the team to the tournament. This broke my heart and I knew that my time as an un-paid coach at Southern was nearing the end and I needed to make alternate plans.

My coaching career had to wait until I finished my degree in education. Even though I could of have earned a degree in engineering by taking a semester of classes, I chose to change my major to Physical Education. The counselors told me that I would have to take 16–18 credits a semester and it would still take me 2 ½ years to graduate—a price I was willing to pay. When I eventually graduated, I had over 180 credits instead of the usual 126.

During my second year of coaching at Southern, I was put in charge of the whole wrestling program. That year we had the most successful team in Southern Connecticut history. We were New England Champs and qualified seven wrestlers to a Division II Nationals. Again, I was not rewarded for my involvement and the head coach didn't take me to the tournament. There I was, one of the main reasons the wrestling program was so successful and doing it all for free and the coach did not reward me in the smallest of ways—could he *still* be remembering that first night on campus? It was a major time for change.

Luckily for me, New Haven is also the home of Yale University. I had one more year to graduate and I said to myself, *if I'm not going to get paid at Southern, I might as well go over to Yale and help that team out. At least I can put Yale down on my resume'.*

Little did I know or acknowledge it, but God was beginning to do some "serious" work in my life. That is the only explanation for how I got to Yale and how I became a wrestling coach at Yale. The head coach's name was Bert Waterman and as I reflect back, he was one of the finest men I had ever met. Of course, Coach Waterman knew my Dad and knew what I had done over at Southern Connecticut. It just so happened that Yale needed an assistant wrestling coach—a paid assistant wrestling coach. I thought I was in heaven. Yale paid me $1300 for the season and gave me two tickets to all of the Yale football games. When you do things God's way, the benefits are great.

Now, instead of coaching guys that were in college just to wrestle, I was coaching future doctors, lawyers and CEO's of major companies.

That year we had a great team at Yale. We were Ivy League Champions and took fifth in the Eastern Wrestling Championships, the highest place in Yale history. We qualified three wrestlers to the NCAA Tournament and Coach Waterman *took me to the Nationals!* However, I was not completely ready to give up my old habits, I was still a partier. In fact, I almost didn't make it to the Nationals because of partying too late the night before the team left. I missed the plane out of New York and had to catch up with the wrestlers in Chicago. When I walked on to the plane in Chicago, Coach just looked at me and said, "Hi Joe." (My given name is José, but my mom didn't like it too much. I grew up as Joey).

As a result of the success that the wrestling team experienced, when the lacrosse team also needed an assistant coach, my name was brought up. The only difference was that the lacrosse coach was a straight arrow. When he hired me to be his assistant coach, he didn't realize what he was getting. I was still a heavy partier. I think experiences like this, point to God's humor.

That May, I graduated from Southern Connecticut and

had a tough decision. The Yale wrestling coach loved me and wanted me to stay in New Haven. But I hated the cold weather and I needed to start making some money. I was so poor while attending Southern, that I qualified for food stamps. Once a month, you would see me in line at the Social Services Department, getting my food stamps in order to eat.

I began my adult life teaching at the summer Stroudsburg Wrestling camp. While there, I had met Andy Noel, the head coach of Cornell University. He told me about an opening that Ithaca College had for a head wrestling coach. Ithaca was my Dad's alma mater. I thought, *what a great way to make my Dad proud of me by being the head coach at his alma mater!*

They set up an interview and I jumped in the car. I met with the Athletic Director and did such a good job on the interview that he offered me the job right on the spot. I can't tell you the amount of pride I had driving back to Stroudsburg, Pennsylvania. I couldn't wait to tell Dad that I was going to be the head coach at his alma mater.

When I got back to camp, I told Dad, "They offered me the job."

Dad looked at me, and asked, "Well, what did you tell them?"

I said, "I told them I'm taking it, Dad. I told them I'm going to be there."

The Gov looked at me, and walked away. Here I was thinking it was going to be one of the proudest days of my Dad's life, and he didn't even talk to me.

He came back three hours later, and I said, "Dad, what's the matter? I thought you would be happy."

"I don't think you should take the job," Dad said. "I think you should start as a high school coach and work your way up to college."

I couldn't believe it. Once again, I had failed the test in my dad's eyes.

After the camp, I flew down to Florida for the "National

High School Coach's Convention." My Dad told me that if I ever wanted a high school job that all I had to do was go to this convention. My best friend, Jerry Goodfellow and I were walking around the convention. I had a wrestling shirt on when this elderly lady came walking up to me. She asked if I knew of anyone wanting to be a high school coach. I looked at her and said, "Me." My Dad knew of only one wrestling coach in the state of Florida. It just happened to be the same high school that needed a coach. I just thought it was a coincidence, but now I know it was God's plan. When I accepted the job in Florida, the local newspaper wrote that I was a . . ."thoroughbred wrestling coach." I wasn't used to such compliments.

I weighed the options. I would only get paid to coach the Ithaca team, no full time position. It was in a cold city and I hated the cold. While I was still at camp in Stroudsburg, I received a phone call from Florida. The wrestling parents from Martin County High School called to encourage me to come to Florida. They were saying all these nice things and how they would support me in everything I did. I had never heard such encouraging words before. Add that to the Gov's reasoning and I accepted the Florida high school job instead.

I got down to Florida and had a great job at a school that really wanted me. However, I was not completely ready for God's plan and I still was leading a bad lifestyle. Our teams worked really hard and were successful. But when it came to winning the championships, we always took second. It reminded me of my wrestling career. If you work hard, you will be successful, but when it comes to the thing that you want most, it isn't going to happen, especially if you party.

My second year at Martin County was still very good. We were very successful, but my lifestyle was getting me in trouble. This was also the time when my older brother, Mike, had completed his five-year commitment in the Army. He had met some friends on the All Army Wrestling Team and moved to Fullerton, California. Over spring break that year, he invited me to come to California. Mike had friends that were high school wrestling coaches and knew of job openings. I flew out to Los Angeles, California. This was my dream–to live in California. However, that dream was not to come true. The Gov had a triple by-pass operation that same year. I had to fly home and found Dad in the hospital. This was the man I admired most, the man that I wanted to be like. I walked in the hospital and saw all kinds of tubes coming out of his body. How could this happen to my Dad? He didn't smoke, was in good shape and didn't miss a day of school for over ten years. I remember, he had a scar on his leg from his heel, up to his groin. His chest was black and blue from the doctors sawing his ribs apart. To see the Gov like that made a huge impact on my life. I knew I had to do something a little bit different than teaching business math and coaching high school wrestling. There had to be more to life. This incident would become more profound to me as time passed.

Shortly after that, my brother got a job in Salt Lake City, Utah and he was moving away from Los Angeles. It was time for me to move on also. I found myself on the way to San Diego, California. San Diego was a place where a bunch of my high school friends lived.

I decided after dad's triple by-pass open-heart surgery, it was time for me to stop teaching for a time and help people more. I wanted to educate people to the risk factors associated with heart disease. Little did I know that *living the right kind of lifestyle* would be part of my formula for a blessed life.

When I moved to San Diego, I met up with one of my oldest friends named Bobby Antonacci. Bobby's mom died of heart disease and, he too, used his experience to motivate others. He owned a company that evaluated people's physical fitness and identified their risk factors for heart disease. I worked for Bobby over the next four years. Through that job, I found that I had a gift for lecturing and really enjoyed speaking in front of people. Bobby was just starting his business and couldn't pay me much. I became bitter with Bobby because he had a nice house and felt I wasn't being treated fairly. I was still partying and my girlfriend from Florida had moved out with me. Little did I realized that this was all part of God's plan.

When God has a plan for your life and you are ignoring or unaware of that plan, He will begin to tap on your shoulder to get your attention. My first tap came in the form of my younger sister. She was the only Christian in our family and she confronted me about living with a girl. She pointed out that I was living in sin. At the time, I couldn't understand what she was talking about. However, the "tapping" became stronger. My life was focused on the party and my work was a means to pay for my lifestyle. Therefore, when I was hardly making any money, I was really mad at Bobby Antonacci and surviving became an issue. At the time, I was so thankful for my New York friends because they would party with me. These were friends that either played football or wrestled for the Gov—all partiers, unlike Bobby.

Chapter 5

ARE YOU LISTENING ?
... GOD IS TALKING.
Becoming A Christian

One of many good qualities about Bobby Antonacci was that he was a Christian. In fact, he was the first Christian I had ever met. Bobby was aware of the lifestyle that I led, and he once said to me, "You know, I think you need to change your life. I believe that, if you change, then good things would happen to you."

I wasn't, however, prepared to believe him. He was married and everything good *was* happening to him. One day, Bobby came to me and said that the girl he married had physical problems. The doctors told her that she would never be able to have children. However, this did not stop Bobby from trying or from having faith that God was in control. Bobby and his wife were strong Christians and, the next thing you know, Bobby's wife became pregnant.

Bobby's first son, Tony, was born. When the doctors delivered Tony by caesarian section, they examined Bobby's wife and were amazed. They looked at Bob and said, "We don't know how this happened, but I just want to let you know right now, you'll never be able to have children again."

Bobby laughed and said, "Yeah, right! That's what you told us the first time."

A few years later, Bobby shared that he and his wife

were expecting their second child. Again, the doctors looked on in amazement when the boy was born. I asked Bob how this all could happen—the doctors said that she could never have children?

I remember that moment when Bobby looked at me and said, "José, my wife and I are Christians. The Bible says that if you pray to God, asking him for things, believe in Jesus Christ and let Him be your Lord and Savior, that God will answer your prayers. I know that you've been going through hard times. If you change your life, God will give you all the things that you ever wanted."

Step One: Fellowship

I think it was at that moment that I realized how tired I was. Tired of the lifestyle, tired of no success, tired of no plan— I was ready for a change and allow God's involvement. I was raised a Catholic and grew up living across the street from a church. However, I never listened to what the priest was saying and I would count the minutes until Mass was over. With this past knowledge, I knew there was no way God would help me or answer my prayers. *How could God forgive me for all of the bad things that I have done in the past?* I just didn't believe Bobby. However, God placed a burden on my heart and I knew that the first thing I needed to do was go to church. This began my search for a Christian church.

While riding my bike around Pacific Beach, I came across a little church called the Pacific Beach Christian Church. It only seemed right that if you wanted to become a Christian, you should attend a Christian church, right? One Sunday, I walked in and signed my name in the guest book. The preacher was an old man with bad arthritis, confined to a wheelchair. All the people there were older people. At the end of the first service, the preacher looked at me and said, "José! We are so happy that you came today, and we hope that you'll make Pacific Beach Christian Church your home."

I thought, *how could he know my name?* I forgot that I had written my name on the guest list as I walked in. It was amazing how the people treated me so nice at the church, like they really cared for me.

Step Two: Read the Word

The next couple of months, the people at that church embraced me and made me feel welcome. They gave me a Bible, which I started reading. I had never read the Bible before and I found that I had a hunger to read all the time.

On one particular Sunday, all the single women were especially happy. I thought it was because of my attendance. Little did I know that their happiness was brought on because their Social Security checks had just arrived? You see—all of the single ladies were over 65!

As you begin to clean up your life by changing your actions and behaviors, God will reward you and provide what you need at that exact moment. I needed that little church full of loving people. I needed to know that I was worthy of forgiveness.

Step Three: Have Faith

The next thing you know, I didn't have a job. I didn't have a car and I was living in the worst part of the city you could imagine. I didn't even have a girlfriend. The girl I was living with got tired of me and moved back to Florida. One Sunday, the Pastor looked right at me and gave an invitation to come forward and give my life to the Lord. I felt God picking me up and walking me to the front of the church. He continued to ask if anyone would like to give their life to the Lord and if so they could do it right, then and God would forgive their sins completely. The year was 1985 and I was making the most important decision of my life. That decision to respond to the invitation not only changed my actions but my desires as well. No longer did I desire to party, curse, or hang out with people that did these things. For nine years, I got high almost every day, I looked for shortcuts to success, I had made excuses or blamed others for my lack of success—but, on that day in 1985, I walked away from that lifestyle. I was born again!

Step Four: Growing in my relationship with God

Pacific Beach Christian Church was great. The people were very caring, but I needed more. I needed younger people to fellowship with. As I asked around, one of my co-workers at Bob's company invited me to his church called Horizon Christian Fellowship. He shared that he went to a church where you did not have to worry about how you dressed. You could come in shorts and T-shirts. The pastor was a young guy and very funny. He made going to church enjoyable and the music that they played was up beat. They even had rock bands playing. It was an invitation I couldn't pass up.

Once again, God was tapping me on my shoulder. My sister, Jacque who was living in Portland, Oregon called me shortly after my friend invited me to church. She could not stop talking about this pastor, who was originally from Portland. How he had moved down to San Diego and I should try to look him up. Little did I know that this was the pastor of my friend's church and the beginning of a life altering experience.

I was in for a surprise at Horizon Christian Fellowship. The pastor was a young man from Oregon and he was a comedian. Laughing in church was something I had never experienced before. The pastor was Mike MacIntosh. The first day I attended, Mike told the story about how he was a high school wrestler. He wrestled a boy named Willie Bowles, and they bumped heads and both got knocked out. I couldn't believe it, a young, funny pastor and an ex-wrestler. I could not believe my luck and planned to come back the following week.

The next Sunday, Pastor Mike was not there. The assistant pastor was preaching and his name was Sean Mitchell. Sean had just asked his girlfriend to marry him. He was jumping up and down when he told everyone that his girlfriend said, "Yes," that she would marry him. I had never seen anyone so happy that he was going to get married.

I said, *Man! I want it like that someday!*

In Sean's sermon, he told the story about "40 wrestlers for Christ." Sean spoke of Emperor Nero having bodyguards that were wrestlers. These wrestlers were also followers of Jesus Christ. In fact, they gave their life up because of their belief in Jesus Christ, instead of worshipping Nero. I thought to myself, "Wow! Can you believe that?—The first week Pastor Mike talks about wrestling. The second week Assistant Pastor, Sean Mitchell, talks about 40 wrestlers for Christ. This is my church. This is where God wants me."

Pastor Mike talked about baptism. Even though I became a born-again Christian, I was not baptized. Horizon was planning an event—a baptismal service down at the bay, so I went down to be baptized There were three pastors, standing in the water baptizing people who had made decisions for Christ. I had my two younger brothers, Rick and Manny, watching me. They didn't understand because we had been baptized as Catholics, but we didn't have any choice about it. Now as a Christian, I was making a choice to change my life and follow Jesus.

Pastor Mike said, "You can go to any of the pastors, and they will baptize you." Of course, I wanted to be baptized by Pastor Mike. He was the ex-wrestler and I wanted to be baptized by him. As I walked into the water, Mike was waiting for me. I started weeping and told Pastor Mike how his sermon about being a high school wrestler really touched me, because I was a wrestler. Pastor Mike told me that I was going to be a teacher and get back into coaching wrestling. These prophetic words about my future would soon become reality.

Miracles started happening in my life. My parents came to visit me and they knew something was different. God gave me the courage to with stand the peer pressure of using drugs, of being influenced by friends that did not have my best interest at heart. This was courage that I had never had before and my parents saw the change.

My Dad woke me up one morning and said, "Let's go. We have to get you a car."

We went around the corner to the local car dealership. I didn't have the money to buy a car, so the Gov helped with the down payment. I couldn't believe it. At 31 years of age, I finally got my first new car. It was a nice Mercedes. At the time, this type of car was only for "cool people". Honestly, my car was really a Toyota Tercel, but to me, it was a Mercedes. For years, I would fool my wrestlers by telling them I had a Mercedes. I would ask them to go to my car and get something.

"It's the red Mercedes with surf racks on it," I would tell them.

With my new car, I would drive around San Diego looking for a high school where I could teach. I remember one day as I was driving around I tuned into a Christian radio station, and heard "Focus On The Family". This became my station of choice and I would listen to "Focus On The Family" every morning while driving around. I would hear stories of how God changed people's lives. For the first time, I heard that God had a specific plan for my life.

As I read my Bible and learned how God's plan for my life was based upon grace and obedience, I began to see the fruit of His spirit. His plan was taking form—remembering what Pastor Mike had told me when I got baptized; I continued to look for the high school where God wanted me to coach and work. That place appeared one day while I was driving around. I was amazed at how beautiful it was. It had two outdoor swimming pools, two wrestling rooms and they just happened to need a wrestling coach. It was called, Mt Carmel High School and later I learned that Mt. Carmel meant "God's vineyard".

God Rewards the Faithful

So now I have a job and a car. Man! My next desire was a girlfriend. As my faith was growing, I knew that God had the perfect girl waiting for me. However, God wanted to make sure that I was mature in my walk with Him therefore He tested my faith by making me wait. In fact, right next to my bed I had a scripture that said:

"Godliness plus contentment equals great gain."
1Timothy 6:6

I was finally living a godly life. I was content with the things that God had given me and I knew more than anything else that God had the right girl out there for me. Of course, *my* plan was different than God's. I was going to meet a California girl with long, blonde hair who loved to go to the beach, and she would be my wife.

God made me wait. He tested my patience and after three years, I was loosing a little bit of that patience. My friend, Bobby Antonacci, called and told me that he had the perfect girl for me. She exercised a lot, was very active, loved the Padres and wanted me to call her. I called the girl up, all excited. I was going to take her to the nicest restaurant, maybe to a play and try to really impress this girl. Well, the girl turned out to be a real jerk. I took her back to my apartment after we went out to dinner. She was such a jerk that I walked to the front door, opened it up and asked her to leave.

She looked at me funny and said, "What? What did you say?"

I said, "You know, we're not the same kind of people. Things just aren't going to work out. Could you just please, leave?"

As she was walking out the door, she was cursing and calling me every name in the book. When she went out, I closed the door and just laughed. I knew that she wasn't the girl God had chosen for me.

The very next day, when I arrived at school, the football coach was waiting for me. He tells me of a new substitute teacher at our school that is "really nice."

"Would you like me to introduce you to her?" he asked.

I said, "Coach, last night I had the worst blind date in my life. Thank you very much, but I'm going to take care of myself. I don't need anyone hooking me up."

He said, "Okay, but if you want to meet her, I'll introduce you to her."

I said, "Thank you, but no thanks."

As I sat in my second period classroom the door opened up and in walks two of my senior wrestlers.

I said to them, "Fellas, I can't believe the Varsity football coach is trying to set me up with some substitute teacher."

My wrestlers said, "Yeah, Coach. That's the substitute teacher whose class we just walked out of."

I asked, "Is she nice?" (overlooking the fact that they had just rudely walked out of her class).

They said, "Yeah, Coach. She's real nice."

So I said, "Okay. Go talk to her for me."

So the two wrestlers leave the room and went back to their original classroom. Five minutes later, the guys come back and they say, "Aw Coach, she's really nice. Her brother was a wrestler in Nebraska. She loves wrestlers. She's really cool, Coach. You should talk to her."

I said, "Okay. Go tell her to call me."

My two wrestlers run out the door and they go back to the substitute's room. They come back five minutes later and say, "Sorry, Coach. She says you have to call her."

"Ok. Go get her telephone number for me."

Out the door my boys go. Five minutes later they come back with her telephone number. At lunchtime, I walked in the teacher's lounge and asked the football coach to point this teacher out for me. Remember, my plan was to have a California girl with long, blonde hair. When I looked, I just saw the back of her head. She had short, black hair, and was from Nebraska. Not exactly the vision I had in mind for my dream girl!

I called her up (anyway) and invited her down to the beach where I lived. She was telling me how physically active she was, so, I was going to see exactly how active this girl really was. I told her to bring her bike and that we were going to go for a little bike ride. I had been doing triathlons, so bike riding was easy for me. I took her on a 24-mile bike ride around San Diego. I had a nice triathlon, racing bike and she was on this old beach clunker. To Stacey's credit, she did not complain once.

After our bike ride we went out to dinner and a movie and had a great time. Little did I know, that this was the girl God had planned for me to meet and eventually marry. I am so lucky to say that the substitute teacher has been my wife for the last fifteen years. I tell everyone that I've coached champions in wrestling, received coaching honors that I really didn't deserve, but there is nothing compared to the happiness I had, June 30th, 1990. That was the day Stacey Stauber said she'd be my wife. It's hard to believe that this girl is my best friend. She takes care of me and understands what wrestling is all about. During the season, she is always there for me. She understands that my purpose in life has been to help kids get through the disappointments of life through the sport of wrestling. I thank God everyday for the perfect girl He provided for me.

God knows our gifts

God has also given us two daughters. Serena and Toya are two little girls that make coming home so much fun. Whenever my team would get our butts kicked in wrestling or I'm having a hard day, what a blessing to hear your daughters say, "I love you, Dad" or "Let's go surfing, Dad." I'm so blessed to have two daughters and God knew what he was doing. If I had

had sons, you know I'd have them out wrestling and everyone would be miserable. Thank you, God.

In 1993, I also learned about the "grace" of God. *Wrestling USA* magazine named me the "National Wrestling Coach of the Year." I have always understood justice. If you do something wrong, then you deserve the consequences. But grace is getting something you don't deserve. Usually, one has to win big championships in order to receive an honor such as "Coach of the Year." Therefore, it was embarrassing to me because my teams had never won a big championship. In fact, we were not even League champions! I was also embarrassed because my dad had some of the best teams in the country and he never won this award. But again, I learned that my plan is not the same as God's plan.

God blesses those that obey

As I look back over my life and reflect on where I am today, I realize God has blessed me beyond wonder. I have a wife who loves and cares of me, healthy children and a job I look forward to everyday. I have a home far beyond my wildest dreams (houses in San Diego are very, very expensive—getting ours was a miracle). Now with the coaching award, and the interest in this book, doors are opening and allowing me to share how God has changed my life. I can honestly say that God has given me everything I have ever wanted.

PART TWO

Keys to Success

- **DEDICATION**
- **EDUCATION**
- **AFFILIATION**
- **LIVING A GOOD LIFESTYLE**

Chapter Six

DEDICATION
The Six Components of Dedication

The word dedication, is used so often, that the meaning can be misleading. All of the most successful people I have ever met or read about had one common characteristic—dedication. Dedication can be broken down into *six* categories to better understand the broad use.

1)   The first area of dedication is **desire**.

One cannot have desire unless you first have a dream. The dream should give you a hunger to achieve. I call it the *overwhelming desire to win.* If you don't have the desire, no motivational speech in the world will help you achieve your goals. It all starts with a dream. You see something or someone and you imagine yourself in their shoes. You can be blessed with a great physical body and quickness, or maybe the ability to pick things up faster then the average person. But if you don't have that dream, the desire to succeed, success will be harder to attain. The desire to achieve is what motivates all people. Its desire that makes the wheelchair athlete continues to compete. Its desire, when a boy desperately wants to please his dad or coach. They all had to prove to themselves they could do it. When your mind is getting weak and it tells you to slow down or it's not worth it, your overwhelming desire to succeed will pull you through.

Dan Gable was the legendary wrestling coach for the University of Iowa Hawkeyes. He holds the distinction of being the most successful coach in any sport. In 21 years of college coaching, his teams won the NCAA's 15 times. Many felt that Dan Gable was able to achieve this success because of his recruitment practices, and in some respects this is true. Coach Gable recruited young men who had the "desire" to wear the Iowa singlet and to focus on what was needed to become "National Champions."

2) Once you have a desire or a dream, you must have a **plan**.

There are many ways you can design a plan. My Dad always taught me," If you want to be a millionaire, you have to learn from other millionaires. If you want to be successful, the best way to learn is from other successful people." It helps if you can have other people or experts helping you design a plan to carry out. Teachers, coaches or mentors are all examples of plan builders. I love coaches who are always trying to learn new and better things about their sport. Attending clinics, reading books or just watching successful will separate you from the average. I was lucky enough to be around some of the greatest people while growing up. I saw what worked for them and what didn't. The ability to learn from others is an important step to achieving success. Only people who are truly dedicated to their desire ever come close to attaining success.

3) A major part of any successful plan is the ability to **work hard.**

The bottom line is: you have to pay the price. Nothing good comes in life unless a lot of hard work has gone into it. Short cuts may get you temporary success-but when it comes to getting the thing you really want-without hard work-it will never happen. My Dad always told me, "The harder you work the luckier you will be." One of the reasons steroids and performing enhancing drugs are so popular is because people don't want to put in all the hard wok necessary to become champions. Walter Payton and Roger Clemens, both Hall of Famers, had one thing in common. During the off-season, they would train harder than everyone else. Vince Lombardi said," the dictionary is the only place where success comes before hard work."

4) **Discipline** is essential to any plan.

Its one thing to have a dream or a goal and figuring out a game plan will help you reach that goal. But if you don't have the **discipline** to follow that plan, you can forget about it. You just can't work hard occasionally. In athletics or business, you have to train consistently. A good Christian is like being a good athlete. They both have end goals in sight. It takes discipline to keep up your workout schedule, just like your time with the Lord. Starting your day reading the Bible and praying consistently takes discipline. The Bible is God's game plan, the one I want to follow!! Vince Lombardi said, "A disciplined person is one who follows the will of the one who gives orders." The people who are successful and accomplish great things are those who are willing to discipline their lives and maintain their health.

5) Hard work's constant companion is **sacrifice.**

If you are serious about reaching your goal, you must be willing to work when you would rather be doing something else. Everyone likes to win or be successful. But who wants to put in all the hard work and sacrifice it takes. Everyone saw Lance Armstrong win the Tour de France, the most grueling athletic event known to man. Lance does not win the race in July, like most people think. He wins the race in the off-season. When he is out on the same course, while nobody else is around, he still works hard. Putting that extra effort in when he is all alone makes him win when the whole world is watching.

6) **Enthusiasm** is the last category, under the term dedication.

Finding something you absolutely love to do is so important in being successful. I didn't enter teaching because of my father's desire or approval. In fact, it was just the opposite. I entered the teaching profession because I love to teach. Surround yourself with people who love their jobs. If you don't enjoy what you are doing, it will be difficult to give the extra time, effort and devotion to takes to be a success. Babe Ruth loved to hit, just like Jack Nicklaus loves to play golf.

As you read these next stories, you will see examples in the six areas of dedication.

STORIES OF DEDICATION

Mike Champagne

*Sacrifice comes when your priorities
are aligned with your goals.*

You shouldn't have to tell someone how badly you want something—it should be apparent from your actions. Mike Champagne comes to mind. Mike had a learning disability called autism. His brain could not process spoken information as quickly as a typical athlete. For a wrestler, this is a big disadvantage. When I would say, "Circle left," Mike would have to think, left? As an athlete, he was not blessed with much talent or strength. Despite the adversities Mike faced, he made up for them with his hard work and determination. First to practice, last to leave, determined and focused, Mike approached his goals by out training his opponents. At times I would feel guilty, heading home for dinner knowing Mike was still working. Mike's desire to achieve set him apart from others. We ask all of our wrestlers to climb the ropes five times everyday, to improve their grip strength. Mike added his own expectation of climbing to ten times.

One night, Mike called his Dad to come and get him after practice. When his Dad arrived, he found all the lights of the wrestling room off. After searching the school and wondering where his son might have gone, he returned to the wrestling room. It was at that point he heard a grunting noise coming from the ceiling at the far end of the room. Looking up, he saw his son, Mike, at the top of the ropes.

Mike yelled down, "I'll just be a minute, Dad. I have three more to go."

His Dad, chocking back tears of pride, said "Okay, Son."

This dedication to hard work won Mike the nickname of "Psycho" around campus. He could be seen doing push-ups at every stoplight while jogging around the community. Running to school in the morning with his 50-pound backpack, was nothing out of the ordinary for Mike. He qualified for the state championships in his senior year. During his second match, Mike dislocated his elbow. He didn't want to end his high school career, without giving 100%. Mike asked the trainer to tape up his elbow to see if he could continue. Wrestling with only one arm, Mike tried his hardest, but couldn't beat his last opponent. As he walked off the mat, his head dropped down in disappointment. I thought of the countless hours Mike put in trying to achieve his goals. I walked to the edge of the mat, trying to think of words, which would let him know how I felt. I hugged Mike and told him how proud I was. We cried together, knowing that life was not always fair.

Most of the time, especially in individual sports, you get out of it what you put in. You don't have to worry about someone blocking for you or passing you the ball. Mike was one example when the success, or outcome *didn't* equal the amount of work he put in. However, success did come to Mike. He went on to be a college All American and now serves as an officer in the United States Marine Corp. Wouldn't you want to follow someone into battle who leads by example? Mike has the desire to achieve whatever he sets his mind to accomplish. His attitude and work ethic has paved the path to his successes.

DAN GABLE AND LARRY OWINGS

*Don't be afraid to fail. Give it everything you
have and don't worry what others will think.*

When I was in eighth grade, my Dad came to me and said, "Would you like to go to the NCAA Tournament and watch Carl Adams wrestle?"

Carl Adams is the greatest wrestler my Dad ever coached. He was a New York state champion and received a full scholarship to Iowa State University. Carl became the first freshman All-American and was a two-time NCAA champion.

One of Carl's teammates at Iowa State was a man named Dan Gable—the most talked about wrestler in our country at the time. Gable was a three time state champion in high school and two time defending NCAA champion. He never lost a match in high school or college and this tournament was his final college tournament. When I knew I had a chance to go out and watch Carl wrestle along with Dan Gable, I jumped at the opportunity. Dad told me if I could raise $100 that he would pay the rest to fly out to Chicago for the tournament.

I had a goal and now I needed a plan. I started doing whatever I could to raise the money. I started selling candy. I'll never forget, I went door-to-door, selling "Mrs. Leland's Chocolate Pollywogs." I sold wrestlers' socks and beanies with our school colors. I would get on a small typewriter, print up the starting line-up for the Varsity matches and sell them for 10 cents each. I wouldn't eat lunch, so I could save the thirty-five cents my Mom would give me. My plan worked and I was on my way to the Nationals.

Upon arriving in Chicago, we picked up the newspaper and the headlines read, **"Owings Comes Down To Wrestle Gable"**. It was a story of a wrestler from the University of Washington named Larry Owings. The year before, Larry Owings went down a weight class, just so he *wouldn't* have to wrestle

Dan Gable. After he was eliminated from the NCAA's, Larry Owings said, "This is baloney. Next year, I'm going whatever weight class Dan Gable is at, and I'm going to beat him." His teammates at the University of Washington thought Larry was out of his mind.

The tournament started and all eyes were on Dan Gable and Larry Owings. Gable had five matches prior to the finals and he pinned all five opponents. Larry Owings had four matches going into the finals, and he had four pins. The crowd was filled with anticipation and could hardly wait for this match.

Dan Gable had not lost a match going back to his high school days. His record was 180 wins and no losses. He was famous for his grueling workouts and the good lifestyle he led. Gable would run to classes on the Iowa State campus with ankle weights on. He would carry his books on a rope and shoot take-downs on them while walking around school. Instead of warming up his neck and bridging on the mats, Gable would bridge on cement. Practicing with teammates 50 pounds heavier then him was the norm. Now, it came down to this match—the last collegiate match of his career.

Before the finals started, the Iowa State wrestlers came out on the mat for warm ups and the arena went wild! Iowa State had robes as part of their uniforms and Gable *threw* his off before he warmed up. One thing was different in this match for Dan Gable. He doubted himself for the first time ever. Instead of being confident of his work ethic, Gable was worrying about how good the guy Owings was. Everyone at Northwestern University field house was on their feet for the entire match. Larry Owings wrestled the match of his life and beat Dan Gable, 13 to 11.

The referee for the match was Pascal Perry, a man from Long Island who knew the Gov. For years I was angry with Perry. I didn't think he did a good job refereeing the match. I felt that he gave away some back points that Owings didn't deserve.

But after watching a videotape of the match years later, I realized that Owings *did* earn those back points.

At the awards ceremony, Dan Gable received a five-minute standing ovation. I had never seen anything like that in my life. Gable stood on the victory stand, crying with his head down. The crowd continued standing and cheering for Larry Owings, but for only three minutes. When it came time for the end of the tournament awards, of course, Larry Owings was named the Outstanding Wrestler. The "Most Pins in the Least Amount of Time" award went to Dan Gable. Another unbelievable chapter of the night was about to happen.

When the awards for the team title were being handed out, the Iowa State team was standing on the far end of the arena. When the announcer said, "NCAA Champions–Iowa State University", the whole team picked up Dan Gable and carried him on their shoulders. They walked across the arena floor, carrying their fallen hero, with 15,000 people applauding. You didn't know whether to cheer or cry. This 8th grader cried! Gable pleaded with his teammates to put him down and finally, in the center of the mat, they obliged. They walked the rest of the way and got the team trophy. It was an unbelievable event for a young boy to see.

You can never learn anything by *always* succeeding. Everyone will fail and stumble at times, but the main thing is to get back up and continue to strive toward being the perfect person God wants you to be. With the desire to accomplish a goal and the determination to do what is needed, disappointments will be overcome and treated as an opportunity to learn. How did Dan Gable take that defeat? He trained even harder. Gable went on to win the Olympic Gold Medal without any opponent scoring a single point on him. He later went on to be the most successful coach of any sport known to man. The University of Iowa's wrestling team was the dominant team in athletics. I would join the Hawkeye Wrestling Club every year, just to hear Dan Gable give victory speeches after winning the NCAA's. It proved that anyone could be beat. Larry Owings proved that if you believe in yourself enough, you could even do the impossible, like beating Dan Gable.

Bobby Antonacci

You can't just have a dream, you have to work hard. Without the hard work, all you will have left is just a dream.

Nobody lifted weights in my high school. We didn't even have a weight room. We had a Universal Machine in the corner of room but nobody knew how to use it. But I did have one friend that lifted weights. Every night, Bobby Antonacci would go down in the basement of his house, look at the muscle magazines and would practice bench pressing. He only weighed 125 pounds, but could bench-press 325. He knew how to use his strength to his advantage. That's why he was a two-time New York State wrestling champion and All American at Iowa State.

When he went to Iowa State, he became a Christian, something that we had never heard of before. Bobby was probably the most competitive person I ever met. When he would teach at summer wrestling camps, Bobby had to find a way to earn extra money. Since he did a lot of push-ups for his training, he had an idea of how to earn more money. He would bet the high school wrestlers that he could do 1000 pushups in 30 minutes.

Of course, no one at the camp believed that he could do it.

Bobby said, "Here's what we'll do. If I can do 1000 push-ups in thirty minutes, you give me a dollar. If I can't do 1000, then I'll give you two dollars back."

Well, most kids thought that was a pretty safe bet.

Bobby proceeded to do 1000 push-ups in thirty minutes, got a dollar from every camper and walked out that week with 300 extra dollars!

When the next group of campers came in, Bobby would sit them all down and say, "I bet I can do 1000 push-ups in thirty minutes."

Some of the kids heard of Bobby's push-ups the week before and said, "Hey. We heard you did 1000 last week."

Bobby said, "Okay. I'll do 1100. If I do 1100, you give me a dollar. If I can't do it, I'll give you two dollars back." So, of course, everyone would throw in a dollar, Bobby would do 1100 push-ups and walk out with 300 extra dollars again.

Bobby was so competitive that he found a book called *The Guinness Book of World Records.* He said to himself, *I have to find a way to get into this book.* Well, sure enough, there was the category, "Most Push-ups in Thirty Minutes". After months of practicing, he finally called up the people at *The Guinness Book of World Records* to come down and witness what he was about to accomplish. With 500 people in the gym at Ames, Iowa, Bobby broke the world record and did 1420 push-ups.

Bobby was so strong. While his teammates at Iowa State were warming up for a match, Bobby would do 25 handstand push-ups in the center of the mat. How do you think his opponent felt watching him do that?

Physical discipline requires you to develop your body the way God intended it to be. Your body is a temple and not the "Temple of Doom." Drinking and drugs, along with poor eating habits, destroys your body. It takes discipline to keep in shape and eat the right kinds of foods.

I'm forever grateful to Bobby because he was the one who led me to Jesus Christ.

Pete Galea

Instead of working on your weaknesses,
perfect the gifts God has given you.

Pete and Bobby were the closest of friends in high school.

They were so confident as wrestlers in high school. As sophomores, they were on the Junior Varsity team. But the way wrestling was in Long Island, New York at the high school where Dad coached, your JV wrestler went along with the Varsity wrestler to the county championships.

Pete was beating Varsity guys. Even though he couldn't start on our Varsity, he was beating all the best Varsity guys in the county. Pete had only one move: cross-face cradle. Pete was known as the "king of cradles". So many times I try to tell kids, "You don't have to know a lot of moves. You just have to know a couple of them, but you have to have them perfected."

Pete and Bobby would be in our locker room all the time, making believe they were in the state championships. They would make believe they were the announcers, saying "In the finals at 126 pounds, from Brentwood, Bob Antonacci!" and Pete would do the same.

Well, Pete and Bobby both got scholarships to Iowa State. After a month at Iowa State, my Dad called up Coach Harold Nichols. He asked, "How are my boys doing?"

Coach Nichols responded by saying, "Antonacci is going to be tough. He's very hard to score on, and he's going to be a great wrestler, but Galea–he only has one move. He's not going to be that successful."

Well, little did Coach Nichols know how successful that cradle was going to be? As a true freshman, Pete Galea broke Dan Gable's pinning record and pinned 22 wrestlers. College guys usually don't get pinned, and can you imagine, as a freshman, Pete pinned 22 guys with his cradle? Successful indeed.

Pete went on to be the first four-time Big Eight champion in the history of wrestling. Then, the Big Eight Conference included Oklahoma, Oklahoma State, Nebraska, and Missouri– all tough wrestling schools. In fact, Pete never lost a Big Eight dual-meet in his four years at Iowa State.

One move, perfected, and you can be a champion.

Mike Shannon

Sometimes desire is more important than
talent, or even a healthy body.

The first year I took over as head coach at Mount Carmel, I had a boy named Mike Shannon. Although this boy was
a returning starter and a very hard worker, trouble found him
two weeks before the season started. Trouble in the form of a
girlfriend who no longer wanted to be his girlfriend. This event
broke Mike's heart to the point where he wanted to hurt himself.
It was a few days later when I got a phone call that he was in a
psychiatric hospital suffering from deep depression.

Most wrestlers love milk shakes so before going to see
Mike in the hospital, I went to the local ice cream place and
ordered the biggest, thickest milkshake possible. I then hid it in
my jacket as I walked in the hospital room. Mike and I sat there,
drinking milkshakes as we talked about girls. I was trying to tell
him that he was going to have many, many girlfriends in his life
and God had the right girl set aside just for him, they just had
not met yet. This girl who broke up with him, just wasn't the
right one.

Mike eventually got out of the hospital and came back
to wrestling practice. Right before our first tournament, we had
to have wrestle-offs in Mike's weigh class. Mike was wrestling
off Peter Newman and in the middle of the match; Peter acci-
dentally hit Mike with his elbow. This opened up a cut that was
going to require stitches.

As I walked with Mike over to the training room to have
the trainer take a look at him, Peter was on my shoulder, asking
me, "Coach, does this mean I'm the starter? Coach, does this
mean I'm the Varsity guy for the tournament?"

I said, "Peter! Let me take care of Mike. Let him get to
the trainer and then we'll talk." Peter kept bugging me, "Coach,
does this mean I'm the starter?"

Once I got Peter to return to the room, the trainer told

me what I expected, Mike would probably need six to seven stitches. Off to the hospital Mike went with his parents as I went back into the practice room.

Ten minutes later into practice, Peter sprained his ankle so bad that he could hardly walk and we knew that he couldn't wrestle that weekend. That night I received a phone call from the hospital and it was Mike Shannon. He had just gotten eight stitches in his eye but the doctor said he could wrestle in the tournament if he wore a mask.

I said, "Okay, Mike. We'll find you a mask."

That weekend Mike wrestled with his mask on. He made it all the way to the finals, tearing people up. In the finals, his mask was moving too much and was rubbing across his eye.

He said, "Coach, let me take this mask off."

So we took it off, and Mike eventually wore the guy out with his endurance. The guy had to call time out because he was so tired.

Mike came to the side of the mat and looked at me with a smile, saying "I broke him, Coach."

Mike went on to win that tournament and end his season by become a CIF Champion and a state qualifier. It proved to Mike that despite the problems of a girlfriend and stitches in his eye, his desire to be a champion got him through the rough times.

Beating Ricky's Team

Don't ever apologize for winning. You have worked long and hard and sacrificed much. Why should you let the other person win?

My younger brother Ricky is a high school teacher and coach, living about 45 miles away. Rick coached with me for nine years before taking over a program of his own. During the first couple of years at Chaparral High School, Rick's team and mine would compete in the same tournaments. But it wasn't until 2002, when he thought he had a team good enough to beat mine. In the first tournament of the year, Rick's wrestlers met mine in the finals. My wrestler was winning by 8 points, until his boy came from behind and won the championship. Over come with happiness, Ricky turned towards the spectators from his school and raised his arms in victory, while jumping up and down. You would have thought he had won the Olympics! Being the competitor that I am, I looked at him and thought, "Boy, am I going to get you!" That day, Ricky's team won the championship and beat us by 50 points. The good news was our teams were going to wrestle each other, one on one, the next Thursday.

Rick was very confident, especially because he had 12 senior wrestlers out of 14 in his starting lineup. In his mind, there was no way his team was going to lose. Even the Gov told me my team didn't have a chance to win. But I could not shake this inner voice telling me we had a good chance to win.

It was a very, very close match, back and forth down to the wire. We were losing by nine points with two matches to go. Lucky for me, the last two wrestlers were the hardest working, most dedicated guys on our team.

First was our little 103-pounder, who had gotten pinned by the same kid the Saturday before. Our boy went out with a vengeance and beat the guy, so now we were only down by five points with one match to go. We had our best wrestler out on the mat.

We went to him and said, "Jerome, this is perfect. You're the perfect person we want in this place. All you have to do is pin him, and we win the match."

Jerome went out there on fire. He took the kid down, got him in a cradle and was pinning him. The referee was from my brother's area, so he was very hesitant to slap the mat. Everybody from our school was jumping up and down on the side of the mat, just waiting for that referee to call a pin. Finally, the ref slapped the mat. Our kids went jumping up and down, and I just looked across the mat at my younger brother and said, "Yeah! All right!"

When the other coaches and I got on the bus, we had real serious looks on our faces. We wanted our kids to think we were mad. But we couldn't hold back the amount of joy we had. We smiled, jumped up and down and told our wrestlers how proud we were of them. I was very thankful. One never wants to lose to a younger brother. It was the best bus ride home we ever had.

Don't be afraid to be a winner. Win with class, win with character. You deserve to win.

Barry Davis

*God can turn a trial into a blessing and
use it to draw you into His heart.*

*He can teach you the lessons He intends for you to learn
and give you His peace in the midst of your difficulties.*

The head wrestling coach at the University of Wisconsin is Barry Davis. When Barry was a sophomore at the University of Iowa, he was the number 1 ranked wrestler in the 118-pound weight class. The Hawkeyes were getting ready for the Big 10 Championships being held that year at the University of Michigan. Barry had a regimen that he followed to get his weight down. Being 5 pounds overweight, the night before the weigh-in was no problem for him. But, at the end of the season, Barry was tired and frustrated with making weight. He told himself that he would wake up extra early and try to lose those last 5 pounds before the team headed to the airport. He went to the Iowa locker room at 4 A.M. with plans to sweat off the pounds. After about 15 minutes in the sauna, Barry gave up trying. He got dressed and wrote a letter to his friend, telling him of his actions. The letter read:

"Dave, I can't do it anymore. I know you can win the

tournament without me. Good luck at the Big 10's and the Nationals. Barry

P.S. Don't come looking for me because you will never find me."

Barry walked across the Iowa campus, and headed straight for the local supermarket. A newspaper deliveryman was bringing papers to a stand and noticed Barry walking.

Because wrestlers at Iowa were so popular, the newspaper guy said, "Barry. What are you doing here? Don't you have to leave for the tournament?"

Barry didn't respond and just kept walking. When he got to the supermarket, he realized the store did not open for another hour. Barry was so tired that he went to an apartment complex, next to the store to take a little nap. He was awakened by a loud noise. It was the same newspaper guy delivering to the apartment complex. Barry got up and asked the guy what time it was.

"Five minutes after seven," he said.

Barry saw the cover of the newspaper that said Wide World of Sports would be showing the wrestling Nationals in three weeks.

Barry walked into the grocery store and went straight to the bakery section. Cream filled donuts were Barry's favorite. He knew it was going to be a bad day because they didn't have any made yet. He got the grocery cart and proceeded to fill it with all of his favorite junk foods. Standing in the checkout line, Barry noticed a red Mustang drive up to the store. He thought, *that car looks a lot like my roommates car!*

Suddenly, running into the store was the coach of Iowa, Dan Gable.

Barry looked at Gable and said," I haven't eaten a thing yet, Coach."

Dan Gable asked Barry, "Do you want to make weight?"

What kind of answer could anyone give a coach like Gable?

"Yes Coach, I do."

Gable takes Barry and drives him up to the airport for the flight to Michigan. Barry's parents live 5 minutes from the airport, so Gable thought it would be a good idea to stop and talk with his parents. His parents encouraged Barry and the team and Barry eventually leave for Detroit. The plane had a lay over in Chicago O'Hare Airport. Gable knew time was running short and his wrestlers had to lose the last couple of pounds before the tournament. Speaking with an airline employee, Gable said he was a businessman, traveling with some associates. Could they possibly use the fitness facilities before their next flight? Barry and three other Iowa wrestlers were standing behind Gable. They were not dressed in business suits, but Iowa wrestling workout gear. The manager agreed and allowed the wrestlers into the fitness room. They immediately jumped on the stationary bikes, peddling very fast.

Another businessman was in the area and he was smoking. Barry looked at the man and was so mad that he wanted to scream at him. Gable made sure that Barry didn't say anything to get them thrown out. Five minutes before their plane was scheduled to leave for Detroit, the wrestlers went running out of the facility.

Before leaving the gym, Barry looked at the man who was smoking and said, "Mister, you better watch Wide World of Sports in three weeks because you will see me become a national Champ."

They were the last ones on the plane before it took off. Barry won the Big 10 tournament and headed to the Nationals. After winning the semi-final match and making weight, Gable handed Barry his sweat clothes and a box. In the box was a dozen cream filled donuts, compliments of the Iowa Hawkeye wrestling fans. Barry went on to win the NCAA title 3 times and was voted Outstanding Wrestler in his senior year. He was a two time Olympian and won the silver medal at the 1984 Games in Los Angeles.

Sometimes the encouragement a person gets is the ingredient necessary for success. The extra pat on the back, the "you can do it" inspirational talk can push a person closer to their goal. I just wonder where Barry Davis would be today if Dan Gable hadn't tried to find him that morning.

Noel Loban

A successful person makes commitments, not promises. He listens and respects those superior to him, trying to learn something from them.

When you think of the countries, which produce the greatest wrestlers, one thinks of Russia, Iran and the United States. One of the last places known for the sport of wrestling would be England. However, along came Noel Loban. Born in Wimbledon, Noel moved to the United States when he was 12 years old. His Mom had a sister living in Long Island, who had different ideas on how kids should spend their free time. When Noel's Mom died of cancer, his Aunt took over the role of family leader. The aunt didn't want Noel playing any sports.

The first group of friends Noel had, were a bunch of wrestlers. When he wasn't delivering newspapers, Noel was learning how to wrestle on the front yards of Copaige. His aunt made him quit the freshmen team and because she needed him at home "cleaning the house and doing dishes."

Sophomore year came and Noel heard his name called over the school's loudspeaker to report to the gym. His coach remembered Noel from the last season and hadn't given up on him. His first match was spent looking at the ceiling lights in the high back arch position—wrestling words meaning he was just about to get pinned. Noel's coach applauded him for not getting pinned and showing a lot of heart. This encouragement stuck with Noel through the season. Junior year found Noel on the varsity squad with a couple more moves in his arsenal. It was the summer before his senior year when big changes began to occur for Noel.

Noel sneaked some mats out of his school to practice on. His friend only lived about 300 yards from the school and it seemed the perfect place to train for the summer. Every day, the two would drill moves over and over, building their confidence. As his senior year began, Noel was now throwing guys around that, before, he couldn't touch. He placed second in the League but that was it. The local Junior college was his next stop. Soccer was always Noel's first love. When the college soccer coach didn't give Noel much playing time, it was straight to the wrestling room. Upon entering the room, he noticed the names on the wrestling room wall of all the National Champions were in red and All Americans were in black.

One day Noel asked a teammate, "How does one get his name in red?"

The other wrestler said, "You don't have a chance!"

Noel always trained with the toughest guys in the room. Whether it was running, lifting weights or wrestling, Noel always emulated the hardest workers. He learned by watching the weaknesses of the other wrestlers. His senior year was better but nothing spectacular. In fact, Noel didn't even place in the county tournament. Upon entering the local community college, Noel decided to play soccer instead of wrestle. It wasn't until being cut from the soccer team, did Noel think about wrestling.

His hard work started paying off toward the end of his red shirt year in college. While wrestling in the Regional championship, Noel hit a foot sweep and broke the guy's ankle. The next year, Noel was captain of the team and National Junior College Champion.

Clemson University's coach at that time was Wade Schalles. Wade was one of the greatest wrestlers of all time and loved what he saw in Noel. In his first year at Clemson, Noel beat the defending ACC (Atlanta Coast Conference) champ 12–2. Failing to qualify for the NCAA's, Noel would break into the weight room after hours. With muscle magazines in his hand, Noel would lift for 2–3 hours. As a junior, Noel qualified for the Nationals, but got beat early in the tournament. Sitting in the stands and watching the tournament, was something he swore would never happen again. As a senior, Noel became the first national champion in the history of Clemson University.

His love for wrestling led Noel to focus on the Olympics following college. Having citizenship in England, Noel was encouraged to tryout for their Olympic squad. He went to their national training camp and "spanked" all of the guys around his weight. Because of a lack of quality coaching, Noel wanted to travel to different countries and seek tough competition. Financially, it was very difficult to train when he had two jobs and was just trying to survive.

Having become a Christian, Noel traveled with Athletes in Action, sharing his testimony all around Europe. This experience helped prepare Noel for the 1984 Olympics in Los Angeles. It had been 33 years since England had a wrestling medalist at the Olympics. My brothers, father and I were living in the Los Angeles area at the time of the Olympics. We were the only Americans in the Anaheim Convention Center, who knew Noel had grown up on Long Island. We were Noel's cheering section and, like normal New Yorkers, we were loud.

Next to the Convention Center was a Hilton hotel. My family would go there between sessions and sit by the pool. Since Noel didn't have access to quality coaching during the games, he knew where to go for help. He would come and sit next to my Dad and say, "Okay Gov, let me have it."

Dad would spend the next hour going over Noel's last match and preparing him for the next round. After losing to the American, Noel just had to win one more match and he would medal.

Lucky for us, Noel's match came up right in front of our seats at the arena. Before walking out to the mat for the last period, the Campo men stood and encouraged Noel to, "Go get 'em!"

Noel looked at us and gave us the thumbs up sign, which meant everything was okay. Before we knew it, Noel was an Olympic bronze medalist.

Noel had the ability to learn from others and it helped him achieve success. Noel is the perfect example how God will reward you when you work very hard and live a good lifestyle. He has a beautiful family now and is a high school wrestling coach, sharing his story all over the country.

Steven Neal

It's easy to be mediocre or ordinary, but it takes courage to excel, to be different from the crowd. That's why not many people can do it. The rewards are great, but so are the risks.

The first wrestling tournament of every season, our team competes against many of the local high schools in San Diego. One year, I noticed this tall skinny boy from San Diego High School. I recognized his parents from church and spoke to them after the tournament. The Dad was a basketball player in college and the mom was the family's #1 cheerleader. We would speak after church and a friendship started to grow. I always felt sorry for the boy because his school lacked a qualified wrestling coach. By the time he was a senior, his skills and hard work alone got him to the state championships. I received a phone call from his mom asking if I could sit in his corner during the state meet. It seems his coach didn't want to travel the eight hours for the tournament. I was happy to do it but then learned the high school principal where Steven attended had insisted the coach show up at the tournament. Steven Neal was able to place 4th in the state meet.

My friend, Jack Spates, was the head coach at Oklahoma University and I called him about Steven. Without any scholarship money available, Jack said Steve's only option would be to "walk on" at O.U.

The coaches at California State University at Bakersfield knew of Steven's potential and signed him to a scholarship. Two years later, the Oklahoma-Bakersfield dual meet came down to the heavyweight match. Steven Neal walked out and won the meet for Bakersfield. The Oklahoma coach was ready to slit his wrists when he saw Steve wrestle. Steve went on to become a 4-time All American and 2-time NCAA Champion.

His senior year was one of the greatest years any American wrestler ever experienced. Steve was NCAA Champ, National Freestyle Champ, World Champ and was voted the "Best Wrestler in the World"!

That wasn't the end for Steve. He always wanted to play professional football. Most teams didn't think about him, because Steve didn't play football in college. It would be unheard of, for someone to make the professional level without playing in college.

Steve had a dream and made a detailed plan on how he could attract some attention from the pros. The New England Patriots picked Steven up and now he has three Super Bowl rings. Steven Neal proved it all starts with a dream and follows with a plan. Only people who are truly dedicated to their desire, ever come close to attaining success. With lots of hard work and living a good lifestyle, God will reward you with all the desires of your heart.

Ryo's Sacrifice

When you sacrifice, the rewards will be sweeter when you reach your goal.

My younger brother Rick was coaching our middle school wrestling program. I would watch his practices and look for kids with the unique characteristics of a future champion. One little boy had a muscular body and walked around with a special confidence about him. His good looks helped his self-confidence, especially when the older high school girls asked about him. He had a name, which was also hard to forget. He was called "Ryo". When Ryo came up to high school, he became very popular. Even before our wrestling season began, other students would tell me how Ryo was going to parties. After class one day, I approached Ryo and told him that I had spies. These spies are always watching him and will come to me, whenever he does anything wrong. Ryo's eyes lit up in disbelief. This made him think twice before doing anything wrong, during his next three years of high school.

Ryo was successful on the wrestling mat and his goal was to qualify for the state championships. He knew his chances were slim because his weight class was packed with tough opponents. Ryo's best chance of achieving his goal would come from losing seven pounds and going down to the next lower weight class. Weight loss is the most negative aspect in the sport of wrestling, especially for a growing boy. But the lessons Ryo learned from the sacrifices and hard Ryo was going to do it the right way. work will carry him for the rest of his life. Since I had experience in losing weight the wrong way,

I told Ryo to come to my house on Sunday mornings and we would train together. We would run ten miles, talking the whole time and became very close.

Through dedication and hard work, Ryo reached his goal of wrestling in the state tournament. When he was eventually eliminated during the state competition Ryo walked off the mat with tears in his eyes. I hugged him and told him how proud I was. I had to remind Ryo that it was the *journey* that made it so special, not the *destination*.

Ryo graduated high school and joined the Marines. He served our country by fighting in the Middle East. He told me how much better prepared he was for combat because of the lessons learned from his wrestling experiences.

The main ingredient of hard work is *sacrifice*. Sacrifice comes when your priorities are aligned with your goals. For example, do you wake up and train, while your opponent is sleeping? More importantly, do you make excuses about not going to church every Sunday? Or is going to church your top priority? The correct selection of priorities will help decide your level of success. You just can't do the hard things when they are convenient for you. Willingness to work when you would rather be doing something else has to be part of your strategy. The greater the sacrifice the greater the rewards.

Chapter Seven

EDUCATION
Lessons Learned

The Lord demands your attention and there are times when
we try to ignore the advice the Lord gives us. The good
news is, He knows how to get your attention. He was able to
grab mine through physical challenges and the lessons that each
of those challenges brought to my life. How does He grab your
attention?

Success and what it looks like is such a large category
and the way one becomes successful varies. Although success
may look different for each person, I do feel there are identify-
ing rules a person must follow in order to reach success. The
first rule is the ability to listen to people in positions of authority
~ Learn the Lessons. On our team, the most important rule we
have is; *listen to the coach.* This rule can be applied to life in
general with God as your spiritual, mental and physical coach.

People in positions of authority have the ability and view-
point to guide and instruct your life. Because of this position,
they often see things differently then you might see them. Therefore, it is important to have a mentor or someone whom you trust
and that you seek their advice, which in turn can often provide
direction in your life. Although I have been aware of this rule
since I was a young boy, I didn't always listen to my coach. The
one thing that was different was that my coach not only spent
time with me on the practice field, but he also came home with
me at night. So for me it was twice the dose of instruction and

wisdom that I had to listen too. However, I was at the age that listening to your parents wasn't always the cool thing to do.

I often ask the athletes in my classes why their team lost. It amazes me how they always point the finger to someone else. It was either, "the coach's fault, the defense stinks, or . . . I did **my** job!" We must be honest with ourselves by asking, "Did we give 100% in preparation? In the game?" Don't try to fool yourself. Success comes from acknowledging and learning from our mistakes. Therefore, the only real losers in life are those who refuse to admit their faults.

Pinning Myself

I asked God for strength, that I might achieve. I was made weak, that I might learn humbly to obey.

One of my first matches as a seventh grader was a very memorable one. My dad brought the whole varsity team down to watch me, and I was very confident on winning. I was pinning the boy in a guillotine and the crowd was going crazy when the referee slapped the mat. I told myself, there was no way the kid was pinned. This referee must really be bad because his shoulders weren't flat on the mat. I remember my opponent standing up and cursing at the referee, saying he wasn't pinned. Then the referee said to the kid, "Be quiet son or I'll take the victory away from you!" When I heard those words, I was kind of shocked and didn't realize what was happening. After we shook hands, the referee raised my opponent's hand. There I was, the son of a Hall of Fame coach, standing in disbelief, after pinning *myself!*! It was a very embarrassing moment and hard for me to overcome. My confidence started sinking, especially when I thought of how I was going to explain it to the varsity wrestlers who witnessed it. I found myself lying and making all kinds of excuses and not wanting to go to my Dad's high school practices. My inability to look at the match as a lesson learned, was so reflected in my denial of error.

So many times, all we concern ourselves with is the scoreboard. Instead of being honest and realistic by finding our weaknesses and working on correcting them, we make excuses. The scoreboard is not the ultimate victory. The ultimate victory comes from the inner satisfaction of knowing that you have done your best and gotten the most out of what you had to give. Success is not measured by money or fame, but how you feel about you own goals and accomplishments and the time and effort you put into them.

Dedication To A Goal

Hard work's constant companion is sacrifice.

In junior high school, I found out that other kids were catching up to me athletically. I thought I could be more successful, if I wrestled smaller opponents. That thought process contributed to my decision to go on a diet and lose weight. In eighth grade, I went from nincty-eight pounds down to eighty-four pounds. The will power I had that year was phenomenal. My Mom loved to bake, especially around the holidays. I helped her make 16 dozen Christmas cookies without eating one! I found out that by exercising hard and following a strict diet, my weight would drop. It was a basic weight loss formula that still works today. The success I had during my 8th grade year was a direct relationship to my hard work and dedication.

Recognizing people of authority is another part of the formula for success. Primarily because those people will not always be people that you want to listen to. One of your challenges will be to recognize their authority and take their advice despite what your brain tells you.

The Knee Operation

*I have heard of only one person who
was perfect and it wasn't me.*

During my second month at West Point, we had to do a thirteen-mile *forced march*. Now a *forced march* is in between a jog and a fast walk, while carrying your full combat equipment. We walked for seven miles and then stopped for lunch. At lunchtime, my right knee locked up and I was unable to straighten it out. I didn't want to tell the seniors that I was hurt, so I kept on walking the rest of the 6 miles. Little did I know that having your knee lock up is a typical sign of torn cartilage.

Upon arrival at the hospital, I met another wrestler. The doctors told us both that we would need knee surgery and the operations would take place the very next day. I feel that it is important to know that arthroscopic surgery was not an option in the early 70's. Knee surgery meant knee surgery and a couple of days in the hospital. When the other wrestler and I woke up the day after surgery, a doctor was sitting between our two beds. He told us that we had to go to a place called "physical therapy". I had never heard of that term before and the doctor said I needed to strengthen my knee in order to have the same abilities that I had prior to the operation. The nurses brought two wheelchairs and told us that Physical Therapy was on the first floor of the hospital and we would have to roll ourselves.

Now, we were on the third floor of the Army Hospital, pushing ourselves in these wheelchairs. To get to Physical Therapy, we had to take the elevator down to the first floor. There were two elevators on the third floor, one right next to our ward and another one at the end of the hallway. My friend said, "Lets go down to the other elevator." So we get in our wheel chairs and head down the hallway. Little did we know that before you could get to the second elevator, you had to go down a ramp. We also didn't see the sign on the wall that said, "Don't go down the ramp if you are unattended in a wheelchair."

My friend decided to go down the ramp first. His wheelchair started going faster and faster and SWOOSH, he made it all the way. He stopped his chair, turned around and said, "Okay, it's your turn." I started going down the ramp and about half way down, the back left wheel on my chair locked up on me. I hung a left into the wall and flipped my wheelchair over. I started screaming because the wheelchair landed on the knee I had operated on. The nurses came running down the hall yelling things like, "I can't believe it!" and, "Oh, no, Oh no!" They put me back into the chair and brought me back to my room. The doctor came and examined my knee and discovered that I had further damaged my knee. The result of my wheel chair fiasco was that I would now need a cast on my leg.

At the end of three weeks, the incision made during the surgery was starting to heal. If you've ever had stitches and an incision, you know that as the incision heals, the area start to itch, I mean really itch. Normally, the itching process is no big deal but due to the full cast that I had on, the only way to scratch my incision was to use a wire coat hanger. I straightened out the hanger and slid it down my cast, to itch the area around my stitches. Little did I know that I was actually ripping out the stitches and causing more problems.

When the doctor arrived to cut my cast off to see how my knee and the incision was healing, he was freaked out! The incision on my knee oozed with infection. This resulted in a return to the casting department, a good lecture from the doc and three more weeks of treatment. When I reflect back, if I had just listened to the nurse and followed her directions to the Physical Therapy department, I would not have spent so much time in a hospital bed.

In October 2003, I needed another knee operation. Fears of the first experience floated around in my head and now at 48, I was prepared to listen. However, due to modern medicine, I basically walked out of the hospital and was back at my house for recuperation in under six hours. For my first knee operation at West Point, I was in the hospital for six and a half weeks! I guess the moral of the story is—don't go down a ramp in a wheelchair unattended!

We do need to look back and learn from our mistakes. That's part of the process of confessing our sins and asking God's forgiveness. Forgiveness is God's way of clearing the slate. It then becomes our responsibility to avoid making the same mistake. To grow spiritually, face up to your failures then focus on Christ for the future. "*Forgetting those things which are behind and reaching forward to those things which are ahead. I press on towards the goal. (Phil 3:13–13)*

Being successful is the ability to listen to authority without saying a word despite your mind telling you to do what you want to do.

The Rib Removed

Faith is often built during great trials. It is easy to talk about suffering, especially when it happens to others. It is difficult dealing victoriously when those painful experiences happen to us.

In my second year at West Point, the wrestling season had just started. Within the first couple weeks of practice, I felt this pain in my ribs. In my mind, I thought I might have simply cracked some ribs. In fact, the pain felt similar to an old injury I received in eighth grade while attending a summer camp at Gettysburg, Pennsylvania.

One of the benefits of having my Dad as a high school wrestling coach was that he knew a lot of college coaches. So when the college coaches would have their summer camps, they would invite me to come for free. At the Gettysburg camp, was a coach named Roger Saunders. He was the head coach at Bloomsburg State University and I loved that man. Coach Saunders was funny and he would encourage me. After every session, Coach

Saunders would take me out in the middle of the mat to wrestle. One day, he lateral dropped me so hard that my feet almost hit the ceiling. When I landed on my back, I actually cracked some ribs. I wasn't able wrestle for the remainder of the week.

Therefore, using past experiences, I felt I had a cracked rib and went to the hospital to get it examined. They took an x-ray and gave it to a doctor to read. This doctor was late for surgery, so he looked at my x-rays really fast. He said, "There's nothing wrong with your ribs. Take two weeks off from practice and you'll be fine." So I took the two weeks off and tried to let my ribs heal.

When I resumed wrestling, my ribs started hurting again. This time, I went back to the hospital and saw an orthopedic doctor named Robert Protzman. I'll never forget him because he was an ex-118-pound wrestler for West Point. He was serious and you couldn't joke around in his office. When he took a look at my x-rays he made a very funny face. I knew something was a little bit different! He told me not to practice that day and just go to the training room and get some ice on my back.

This was in November and it was still football season. All the fall sports were going on and our training room at West Point was filled with athletes. The next thing you know, Doctor Protzman comes walking in the training room screaming, "Everybody get out! Get up and get out of the training room!" Everyone looked at him, and since Doctor Protzman was a colonel in the Army, people moved. All of the athletes and trainers started walking out of the room. I stood up to follow suit, when he looked at me and said, "No, you sit down. I need to talk to you."

Right away, I knew something was wrong. I said to myself, *whatever he says, don't say anything; just nod your head and say 'Yes, Sir.'*

Dr. Protzman looked at me and said, "Tomorrow, first thing in the morning, I want you to come into my office."

"Yes, Sir."

He said, "I want you to bring all your books with you."

I said, "Yes, Sir."

"I think we need to send you to a special hospital down in Washington, D.C."

I said, "Okay, Sir."

He said, "The hospital's name is Walter Reed Army Hospital, and there are some doctors waiting for you down there."

I said, "Okay, Sir."

He said, "We think you have a tumor on one of your ribs and the doctors are going to want to take out your rib."

I said, "Okay, Sir."

He had this puzzled look on his face, because I wasn't reacting like he thought I would. He said to me, "Now, don't start thinking that you're nineteen years old and you have cancer and you're going to die."

My eyes light up and I said, "Cancer? Doctor, what do you mean I have cancer? You said I had a tumor."

Dr. Protzman replied, "Well, there are two different kinds of tumors. There are benign tumors and there are cancerous tumors. We don't know what kind of tumor you have."

So, I said, "Okay, Doctor, I'll see you tomorrow morning."

(For the outcome—see below.)

How We Respond To Crisis

*Adversity is part of the process that God uses
to produce good results in our lives.*

In my mind, dieting and losing weight had been the center of my focus since wrestling season had started. Therefore, my brain started to focus on FOOD, not tumors. If I needed an operation, then my season was basically over. So, of course, the first place I headed to was the supermarket. I got every kind of junk food that you could imagine–Twinkies, ding dongs, apple pies, and soda. I went back to my room and started *pigging out* eating. Suddenly, something came to me.

One of the most popular movies of the year was called "Brian's Song." It was a story about Brian Piccalo, a football player for the Chicago Bears who died of a cancerous tumor. The next thing you know, I thought I was in big trouble.

I ran downstairs to the telephone and called home. Luckily for me, my Mom answered the phone. I was crying and saying, "Mom, Mom! I have to go down to Washington, D.C. They said I have a tumor on one of my ribs. They want to cut my rib out."

My mom was an angel from heaven. She knew just exactly what to say in order to calm me down. She laughed and said, "You don't have a tumor. They must have made a mistake looking at the x-rays. Don't worry about it. Just make sure you call back tonight when your dad gets home from practice and talk to him."

I believed my Mom, and I went back to my room, eating my Twinkies and ding-dongs.

After dinner, I called up my dad. He answered the phone and started yelling at me, "What the heck did you tell your Mother? What did you say to your mother to make her cry? I came home and your mom was going crazy. What did you say to her"?

I said, "Dad, the doctors told me that I have a tumor. I have to go to Washington, D.C. to get my rib taken out."

In his normal, strict voice, he said, "Oh, don't worry about it. I'll meet you down there."

The next day, I flew down to Walter Reed Army Hospital. It was 1974 and the Viet Nam War was going on. The Walter Reed Army Hospital was filled with wounded military personnel who were sent there to recover. Army hospitals don't have individual rooms. Instead they have wards with over 100 beds in them.

As I walked onto the orthopedic ward, I started looking at

the soldiers. The first soldier had both legs shot off. The next guy had only one arm. I am looking at these men and asking myself, "What in the heck am I doing here? I must be in trouble."

The next day, I had a pre-surgery conference in this big auditorium. Fifty young Army doctors were waiting for me in the front of the auditorium, watching as I walked onto the stage. The main doctor lays me face down on a table. He starts giving my past history, telling all the doctors that I was a wrestler from West Point, saying how I injured my ribs as an eighth grader. As I was lying there on my stomach, I looked up behind me and there are fifty heads all standing around the table, staring at me. They said that they would have to go right to my spine and cut out my bottom rib.

My next memory is lying in my bed, feeling this immense pain from the operation. As I looked down the ward, I saw this small woman walking toward me with tears in her eyes. It was Mom who had come to comfort and take care of me. Like the Shepherd, who left his whole flock to find the one missing sheep, my mom left her husband and five other kids to take care of me. Luckily for me, it was a benign tumor. My whole family came down to Walter Reed Hospital for Thanksgiving that year.

Tough times teach trust. God uses our difficulties to develop our character. Adversity is part of the process that God uses to produce good results in our lives. Trouble, if it turns us to the Lord, could actually be the best for us.

The Shoulder Operation

*Admitting you have a weakness and not working on it
is just as unproductive as hiding your mistakes.*

I have always had really bad shoulders. My body is torn up from all the years of wrestling and it didn't help that I never used weight training to reduce the risk of injuries. On the first day at West Point, I had to take a "pull up" test. I jumped up on the pull-up bar and did three pull-ups. On my fourth one, my right shoulder popped out of place. It didn't hurt too badly because it had popped out a bunch of times in high school.

I straightened my arms out and went down. The next thing you know, my shoulder pops back into place. I start trying to pull up again—Bam! My shoulder pops out. I knew I had problems because a wrestler with bad shoulders doesn't equal success. Those are two things that don't go well together.

I, however, did not feel the full affect of this until my junior year of wrestling at West Point. Every time I would grab a guy's leg, my shoulder would pop out. I went back to Dr. Protzman, who had helped me with my rib. It was determined that I would need shoulder surgery and he would do the operation. One small bit of information, however, failed to make its way to my ears and that was how painful the recovery was going to be. The rehabilitation of a shoulder operation is very long and painful. I wouldn't want anybody to go through it.

Looking back, if I had had more knowledge about the importance of a well-balanced exercise program, I might not have had as many injuries. Therefore, I pass on to you from my own education and experience, that it is very important that you seek the advice of your coach or trainer to help you develop a well-balanced exercise program. Weight training has proven beneficial to all people, both young and old, no matter if you are an athlete or not.

Biting My Tongue

*"A fool despises his father's instructions, but he who
receives correction is prudent." (Proverb 15:5)*

What is the number one rule on your team? When I
ask kids, I hear many different things: work hard, never give
up, always have good sportsmanship and etc. All these things
are great rules, but I always tell them the number one rule on
our team is "listen to the coach". I tell my wrestlers that when
they listen to me, their chances of getting trouble are drastically
reduced. But when they don't listen, they tend to get in trouble.

When I was in school, there were times that I didn't listen to my coach. I ate dinner with my coach every night because
he was also my dad. One of those times came when I was in
eighth grade and wrestling. At that time, in spite of my Dad's
warnings, I loved to wrestle with my tongue sticking out of my
mouth. Then I met up with an older Brentwood wrestler.

There was a small school in Bay Shore that we used to
go down to every summer and work out a couple of nights a
week. In fact, all the best wrestlers in the county would go there.
It was an old dingy place with hard mats, but the Gov loved it
because of the competition.

One night, Dad saw a boy who was second in the state
championships the year before. He told me, "Hey! Go wrestle
with that guy over there." As I walked out, I knew I was going to
get my butt kicked. As I got in my stance and started wrestling,
tongue out as usual; I shot a single leg takedown. Normally this
would not have been a problem but my workout partner moved
his knee. My forehead hit his knee and, Bam! I bit my tongue. In
fact, I bit my tongue three quarters of the way off. The first thing
I did was run into the bathroom and look in the mirror. To my
astonishment, my tongue fell out of my mouth. It was only held
on by a couple of strands on the left side. It was extremely painful and I knew I needed stitches. So, I grabbed my tongue and
put it back in my mouth and clamped my teeth together, which

was the only way to keep my tongue in. When I re-entered the wrestling room, the Gov met me in the middle of the mat, put his hands on the side of my head and said, "Let me see."

As I open up my mouth, my tongue fell out of my mouth again. My dad almost fainted when he saw it. He said, "All right, let's go." I put my tongue back in my mouth and closed my teeth as I ran to our car in the parking lot. Sitting in the passenger side, my knees were shaking up and down from the pain. I turned that music on the radio so loud in an attempt to drown out the pain. When the Gov jumped into the car and turned the music back down, I grabbed the knob and cranked it back up—at that point, I didn't care what my dad thought.

We walked into the hospital and were met by this little Asian doctor. The doctor said, "Patient! Patient!" and I couldn't understand what he was saying. I looked over at him and he waved for me to come. He put his hands on the side of my head and said, "Let me see." As I open up my mouth, my tongue falls out of my mouth again. He grabs a big needle and proceeds to stick it right in my tongue!

They laid me down on a table, put a sheet of paper over my face and eleven stitches later; my tongue was good as new, or almost. The next day when I woke up, my tongue had swollen up to three inches thick. My brothers felt bad and bought me a "slurpee", but my tongue was so swollen that I couldn't even fit my lips on the straw. My brothers made fun of me saying, "No girl is ever going to want to kiss you."

The good news was that the stitches in my tongue were "dissolvable". After ten days they disappeared. However, there was a piece of dead skin, the size of your thumbnail, on my tongue. That dead skin smelled so bad that my brothers wouldn't even talk to me. The doctors looked at that dead piece of skin and said, "That skin either has to come out, or we're going to have to cut it out."

I looked at the doctor and said, "You ain't cutting nothing out of my tongue".

So I went home and started messing with that dead piece of skin and yanked it out. The next thing you know, I had a big hole in my tongue. I went back to the doctors and they told me that they might have to stitch my tongue back up to close up the hole. Thank God for me, my tongue grew back together. It all happened because I didn't *listen to my coach.*

A wise man learns from his mistakes. The one who refuses to hear criticism has no chance to learn from it.

Sometimes lessons will come in the form of a life event—events that are affected by how "hard headed" you are, how willing to listen you are and/or how well you react. As you grow, you will want to become more independent. Be careful not to confuse independence with being "hard headed" because the result can be costly and life altering.

From Life Events

DAD'S HEART ATTACK AT THE STATE MEET
Life's darkest trial cannot dim the light of God's love.

My wrestling season ends each year at the California State Tournament. In 2003, I had purchased an airplane ticket for my Dad, but he had to fly up later in the day by himself. He was supposed to come in at 6:00pm, after all my coach's meetings were over. My assistant coach and I drove up to the airport (about 45 miles to get there) to find out Dad had taken an earlier flight. He had been sitting in the airport for four hours, just watching people.

Because of a reservation mistake, the closest hotel we could find was 45 miles from the wrestling arena. In order to make the 6 A.M. weigh-ins for the tournament, we had to leave our hotel at 4:30. Dad didn't have any breakfast and the tournament started at 9:00 A.M. . It is important to note that my dad turned 78 in 2003 and had had heart bi-pass surgery twenty years prior and was still trying to live like he was 20 years old.

Both of our wrestlers didn't wrestle well the first round and lost. Being very disappointed, my Dad and I were sitting in the stands, watching the wrestling. Dad having just eaten a healthy snack of a hotdog and a coke, found one of his medication pills in his pocket. The good Lord only knows how long it had been there. For some reason, he decided to take the pill. As we sat there I tried talking to him about the upcoming matches. He was disappointed that both of our kids lost, so we weren't saying too much. We were watching a match, when I said to him, "Dad, we have to wrestle the winner of those two kids over there. What do you think?"

There was no response. Again, I said, "Dad, we have to wrestle the winner of those two guys. What do you think of those guys?"

Because I still got no response, I look over and it looked like he was sleeping in his chair. So I started yelling louder, and louder, "Dad! Dad!"–and still, I was getting no response.

Dad started shaking, like he was having a seizure. I was asking, "Dad, are you okay? Dad, are you okay?" I put my hand over his chest, to feel for any kind of a heartbeat. I thought for sure he was dead. Then, I had to do something I had never done before. I looked behind me, with all my wrestlers' parents sitting there watching me, I yelled, "Someone call 911!"

They called the tournament physician up to see how Dad was doing. He finally opened his eyes, but looked "lost in space". He told me he was going to be sick, so one of our wrestling parents grabbed a big pan just as Dad proceeded to throw up. There were 6,000 people at the arena and no one knew what was going on. Spectators were screaming at us, "Down in front! Down in front!" Little did they know that my Dad was having a heart attack.

The doctor called 911 and right in the middle of the tournament, the paramedics came with the ambulance. They put my Dad on a gurney and carried him out of the arena. I saw the worried look on my younger brother's face as I walked along with the paramedics. Next, I found myself sitting in the front seat of an ambulance with the sirens blasting. I had never done that before, going through red lights and wondering if the cars on the side streets were going to stop. As we pulled up into the Emergency entrance of a hospital in the middle of Stockton, a million thoughts ran through my head and not one of them had to do with wrestling.

As the day went on, Dad got a little bit better. He was constantly telling me to leave him there and go back to the wrestling to coach my kids—which at that point was the furthest from my mind. I had to beg my dad to stay over night for observations. By the time I arrived the next morning, Dad had signed himself out of the hospital. He refused any treatment and his first words to me were, "If we hurry, we can make the semi finals!" He didn't want to miss any more wrestling. Luckily for me, it wasn't time for my Dad to meet the Lord.

*We may have concerns about the days ahead, but we do know that whatever happens, God will always be with us. Worry can do a lot of things **to** you but prayer can do a lot **for** you.*

Taking The Time

No matter what your circumstances, count your blessings.

Mother's Day is the least favorite holiday of all the holidays of the year for me. It's because I lost my Mom to cancer in 1998. You see, my Mom was a smoker. She started smoking when she was little. She didn't understand that the cigarette companies put things in their cigarettes to make it so addictive that it's almost impossible for people to quit.

Mom smoked all but the last five years of her life. She was diagnosed with lung cancer four years after quitting smoking. As stated before, my mom was an angel from heaven. She was a stay-at-home mom for six kids, the wife of a schoolteacher and a coach of four sports, yet, she made us feel like we had everything we could ever want or need.

She was the person who would come and put her arm around us when my Dad was really strict or hard to satisfy. It was Mom who would always tell us that she loved us—loved me! It was my mom, when I got kicked out of West Point, who told me that it didn't matter, that she still loved me. I miss my mom very much.

Mom's life was not easy. She had lost a set of twin boys in between my older brother and myself. She had to financially manage a family of eight on a teacher's salary. But despite the hardship, Mom was our biggest cheerleader. It was Mom who always told me that I was born to be a teacher.

My mom was selfless. She used to make food for all of my friends too. With six kids, you have a lot of friends and I was constantly bringing my friends home to eat. We didn't have that much money to buy food, and my friends would just raid our refrigerator. However, Mom would always find ways to stretch the meals, to welcome the friends, to make time for relationships. One of my fondest memories is of my Mom making some great spaghetti and Italian food. This is also a funny memory because my Mom hated spaghetti, but she loved having a lot of people around the table.

Have you thanked your mom today? Do you need to call your mom? If you're lucky enough to have a mother, you need to tell her how important she is to you. Call her today and tell her you love her, because there's going to come a day when she's not going to be there. You're going to wish you took the time to tell her that you loved her. Call her, write her.

God will reward you for your love and obedience. I was rewarded. I used to write Mom letters all the time. After she passed away, my younger brother, Rick, and I went to Florida with a moving truck to bring my Dad back to California. I remember going into a room that held all of Mom's belongings. Dad could not bring himself to disturb or touch any of her things. As I packed them up, I found a box full of letters from her children. I was so happy to see that the majority of letters were from me, and that Mom had kept them all.

People don't understand how lucky they have it, whether it's the blessing of having a loving mother or just the ability to be alive and walking around. Appreciate what you have, because it's not going to last.

Mike's First Varsity Match

We must learn how to fail intelligently. Once you have failed, analyze the problem and find out why. Each failure is one step closer to success.

My older brother Mike was my hero. I was the President of his fan club and could scream louder than anyone whenever he wrestled. I can remember how excited we were for his first varsity match. It just so happened that he had to face the defending league champion. As wrestling goes, Mike had a problem getting his weight down for the match. If you are one tenth of a pound over weight, you don't wrestle.

In preparation for the match, Mike had stopped eating on the Tuesday prior to the Thursday night match. On Wednesday, Mike started to panic because he was still 3 pounds overweight. Other wrestlers told him that taking laxatives would help him with the last couple of pounds. With that advice, Mike took a couple of the pills only to discover that you need food in your system for the laxatives to work.

Mike eventually made weight for the match and ate a big sandwich before he wrestled. Right in the middle of the match, however, the laxatives started working. I was sitting in the front row yelling like crazy for my brother, not knowing what was happening. Mike upset the defending champ and instead of going back to our team's bench, he headed straight for the locker room.

After jumping up and down and hugging anyone in sight, I went looking for my brother. When I made it to the bathroom, I was hit with the worst smell imaginable. There was poop all over the walls and floor. Mike told me the laxatives hit him right in the middle of the match. He said he never tried so hard, just to get the match over. It was a secret I had to promise never to share with my Dad.

It was confirmed that day and many days thereafter–He was indeed a real stinker! Ha!

I reiterate that this is not the way to win.

_____

In Summary: THINK AND THANK

Be faithful and leave the results to God. As I look back at my head coaching days, I found myself too concerned about the results. I was taught that there are only two columns in life, wins or losses. Many times, even if we won, I wasn't happy with the way we wrestled. It was one of the traits I got from my dad; being hard to please. I always knew I was teaching my teams the right things. By attending coaching clinics, I have always stayed up on the latest techniques in my sport. I always believed we trained hard. We would train twice a day during the season. To me, we were doing what was right. But I would always lose sleep, worrying about what others would think of me if we lost. Instead of building life long relationships with my wrestlers, I would concentrate on wins and losses. I should have followed the saying, "Try your best and let God do the rest."

Now, as I have gotten older, I can't even remember how our teams have done in the last five years.

Selfish ambition is a terrible trait for personal recognition. It can cause you to dominate social situations and insist on telling stories instead of listening to others. We want to be noticed and prominent. God's ways are just the opposite. I need to be content when others are elevated above me. I need to rejoice and give credit to others without insisting on getting it myself. There is no limit to the good you can do, if you don't care who gets the credit.

You can't please God without faith. Think back at some of the things you spent worrying about. Most of those things, you didn't have any control over and the other things never happened. It is easy to get sidetracked by problems that won't matter at life's end, a tight budget, signs of aging and keeping up with the neighbors that have more possessions than you. Stay focused on obeying God. God always gives us what is best for us.

Learn from your failures and never use it as an excuse for not trying. Our previous mistakes do not necessarily exclude us from serving God. Champions of faith are people who have learned from their failures.

Remember what God has done for you and what you can do for others. God specializes in giving new life to those who seem beyond hope. Take time to remember what lessons God has provided for you and then give Him the love and devotion He deserves. Ask the Lord to help you appreciate the value of time. Thankfulness begins with a good memory. Have you ever thought about the many blessings with which God has showered you? Of course you could never name all the physical, spiritual and eternal blessings. But from time to time, it's good to remember with gratitude His many blessings.

Chapter Eight

AFFILIATION AND LIVING A GOOD LIFESTYLE
Stories of How EVERY Choice Has a Consequence

My first couple of years in coaching, I had some wrestlers that worked extremely hard. I couldn't understand why they didn't reach the championship level equaled to the amount of work they had put in. By looking into this deeper, I noticed their lifestyle choices were not always the best. They worked hard in the wrestling room, but would also party hard at night. I finally noticed that the athletes, who led good lifestyles, were the ones achieving their goals.

Reputation is defined as what others think of you. But character is what you **really** are, especially when no one is looking. Being successful takes character. Many people today will "do whatever it takes" to be successful. My opinion is different. I believe that God will reward you if you work hard and do the right thing. It took me many years to figure this out.

Here are a few stories of athletes I've coached and the consequences of their choices.

Aaron Stanton

We must seek the lost and it doesn't take that much effort.

Aaron Stanton was a boy who wrestled for me for four years. When Aaron was a freshman, I was his Health teacher. I can remember walking to my class one day and passing my Mercedes in the parking lot. As I looked on my car, I noticed two hot dogs attached on the antenna. When I walked into the class, I saw two of my wrestlers looking at me and giggling. Aaron and his buddy Jared had this guilty look on their faces. I knew they were the culprits that put the hot dogs on my antenna.

As a coach, I tell many stories with the hope that these kids will learn from them. Aaron remembered my story about how my older brother, right before he graduated high school, looked at me and said, "I feel sorry for you, because you have three more years with Dad." When I looked at Aaron and Jared, they would smile and have their three fingers up, reminding me that I had three more years with both of them. Little do my wrestlers know that I care for them for the rest of their life and not just the three or four years I coach them in High School.

Aaron was a tough kid, a fighter. He didn't like to follow rules, but would rather do things his own way. Even though we constantly preached hard work and good lifestyle, Aaron would do the first part and work hard, but the lifestyle part was something he always had trouble with. Aaron was a partier.

Aaron wasn't a great wrestler. He didn't have that many moves, but as I mentioned, he was a fighter. He was a competitor and always took second at the big tournaments. At the beginning of his senior year, Aaron came to me and said, "Coach, I'm ready to change. I'm ready to give your method a try. I'm ready to work hard but also lead a good lifestyle. I want the rewards that you speak about."

So Aaron changed his life and stopped partying. He would attend our FCA meetings and continued working very hard in practice. The next thing you know, success started coming his way. His success reinforced the philosophy that we preached. Aaron became a CIF champion, Masters Champion and qualified for the California State Wrestling Tournament. These were some of the goals all of our kids have.

At the states, Aaron needed to beat the defending runner-up in order to place in the top eight. We would need some luck in order to beat him. Little did we know, his opponent broke his jaw and was unable to wrestle. As a result, Aaron was a California state place winner.

All the hard work and lifestyle change paid off for Aaron. Someone who never should have experienced such success had just reached his goals. I can't tell you how proud we were of Aaron at that time.

Aaron graduated from high school and decided to attend the San Francisco State University, a tough Division II school that offered wrestling. Aaron "red shirted" his freshman year because he couldn't beat the starter in his weight class. Little did I know that Aaron had reverted back to his partying ways.

That same year, San Francisco State went on to win the Division II National Championships. In the middle of March, I got a phone call from Aaron. Crying on the phone, he told me that he didn't receive a championship ring.

I said, "Aaron, I don't understand. What are you talking about?"

He said, "Coach, when our team won the national championships, everybody in the whole program got a ring, except me." He was crying, calling the coach dirty names. I knew I had to ask Aaron some tough questions.

"Aaron, did you go to practice?"

Aaron responded with, "Oh, most of the time, Coach."

Then I asked him, "Aaron, what kind of lifestyle have you been leading?"

There was silence on the other end of the phone. Like most kids, Aaron couldn't resist the peer pressure and retreated into the party life while in college. Wrestling was never the same for Aaron again. He dropped out of San Francisco State and tried to wrestle again at a community college, but he didn't have the same motivation it took to be a champion. When I would mention San Francisco State, Aaron would always have a bitter taste in his mouth. He didn't think of the consequences his poor lifestyle choices would make.

Closer to graduation, Aaron would come down and see me whenever he could. He was living with a couple of guys that were working in the golf club industry. About a month later, I received some new golf shoes and a couple dozen golf balls in the mail. Aaron wrote a note saying, "Thanks for all that you have done for me, Coach."

Aaron had finally learned his lesson. He remembered how successful he was, living with a good lifestyle. Aaron now was working in a home for foster kids that no one wanted to adopt.

One morning, I got the phone call that all coaches hate to get. Aaron Stanton had just died in a car accident. He was driving back to his house at 8:00 in the morning with two of his friends. None of them wanted to drive because they were all too tired, so Aaron volunteered. There was no alcohol involved, but Aaron chose not to wear his seatbelt. In fact, two out of the three people sitting in the front seat weren't wearing their seatbelts. When the two passengers fell asleep, Aaron fell asleep too. The truck was heading for the center divider when Aaron woke up. He tried to correct the steering, when the truck flipped three times, throwing Aaron out through the front windshield. The only survivor told me how he woke up and looked down the highway, seeing Aaron lying motionless.

One of the hard things about being a high school wrestling coach is when one of your wrestlers dies; they ask you to speak at the funeral. I can remember waiting in line to the funeral home. I had not seen his Mom yet, when all of the foster boys that Aaron had helped, came walking by. The tears in their eyes told me how much Aaron had meant to them. I had to stand in front of 300 people and tell them stories about this 22-year old boy who had just passed away. It was one of the toughest and most sobering moments of my life. I knew that Aaron had come to our FCA meetings as a senior in high school. I pray that he accepted Christ in those meetings and that someday I'm going to see Aaron again in heaven.

We are all part of a rapidly passing scene. That should sober us up and not discourage us.

Rule #1: Fear And Respect The Gov— Girlfriends And Dogs Included

To avoid lying, do nothing that needs a cover-up.

While growing up, I can remember how my Dad was respected and feared. He was not only feared by the wrestlers, but also by the teachers at our school. One day while sitting in the back of my English class, I was exhausted, hungry and tired from cutting weight for the next big match. As I looked up at the door, I saw the Gov's face and boy, did he look mad.

His lips were tightly squeezed together and he made a motion with his finger saying, "Get out here!"

I asked the teacher, "Is it okay if I go talk to my Dad?"

He said, "Yeah, you can go."

As I walked out, Dad looked at me and asked, "Did you do that math homework?"

I didn't do the homework, but I lied and said, "Yes, Dad. I did it."

The Gov grabbed me by the arm and walked down the hall, where the math teacher was waiting. The math teacher was a short man and he was "shaking in his boots."

Dad looked at him and asked, "Did you get that math homework?"

The teacher looked at the Gov and said, "No, Mr. Campo, I did not."

My Dad looked at me ready to kill.

I said to myself, *Uh, oh. You better think of a good one now.* I quickly said, "The teacher was absent yesterday. I put the homework on the substitute's desk. I don't know what the substitute did with it."

The Gov looked at the teacher and said, "Could this be possible?"

Mr. Campanelli looked at Dad, shaking his head, "Mr. Campo, this could be very possible."

Relieved, I looked at my Dad and said, "I'll do it again if you want."

My Dad knew I was lying. He responded by saying, "You're darn right you're going to do it again!"

Can you imagine how life was for me by having the Gov hunt me down for missing homework?

Dad always thought girls were a distraction and he called them "poison". As a senior, I had a girlfriend during football season. One day, she was at my locker talking to me. She looked over my shoulder and saw my Dad walking down the hall. She screamed, "Your Dad is coming!" I looked over my shoulder and saw Dad walking down the hallway. When I turned back, I saw my girlfriend doing the hundred-yard dash the other way down the hall.

We had so much theft at our school in Brentwood; they had to put guard dogs inside on the weekends. German Shepherds and Doberman Pinchers roamed our hallways, trying to deter any would be robbers.

One Saturday night, after winning a tournament, our wrestling team returned to the school about midnight. We went to walk in the doors and there was this huge Doberman Pincher growling at us, showing us all of his teeth. It was like he was saying, "You are not coming in here!" When the dog walked away, Dad said, "Hey! I think I can make it in my office without getting caught by the dog."

Our whole team said, "Coach! Don't do it! You're crazy! The dog is gonna get ya!"

Dad said, "No. I think I can make it."

So, the Gov opens up the door and starts tiptoeing down the hallway toward his office. The rest of our team had our eyes peeled on the window of the door, waiting to see what was going to happen. All of a sudden, we hear "Rrrr, Rrrr, Rrrr!" We see the guard dog going after Dad, ready to attack him. When he got close, my Dad turned around and screamed, "Sit down!" The dog, bam!–sat right down, looking at Dad. The next thing you know, the dog ran away in fear.

We looked at ourselves and said, "Wow! Even the guard dogs are afraid of the Gov!" That was one of the true signs of respect.

Mark Caught Stealing

The cost of obedience is nothing compared to the cost of disobedience.

One day at practice, a rumor was going around our room. I heard that one of our wrestlers had gotten arrested after a wrestling match. I called the boy over and asked him, "What happened? I heard you got arrested."

He said, "Yes, Coach. A bunch of my friends were stealing computers from a school, but I didn't do anything wrong, Coach. All I did was drive the get away car."

I cracked up laughing. I said, "Haven't you watched TV? Haven't you seen people rob banks that have friends driving the get-a-way car? They are just as guilty as the people that robbed the banks."

I found out that he was involved with stealing 100 computers from our school district. The boy got arrested, but then he tried to come to me to tell me how he was going to change his life around. He asked if I could help by writing a letter of recommendation to get him back in our school. He wanted to graduate with the Senior class and wrestle his friends.

I thought about the trouble I had gotten into as a boy and decided to help him. I wrote a nice letter and got him back in school. But when it came time for wrestling season, he decided he didn't have enough time for wrestling.

Mark continues to live a bad lifestyle. He hides from me even today—a sure sign he knows how disappointed I am that the lessons I tried to teach him went unheard. As young men, life is going to provide many crossroads where you will have to make choices and decisions. Each and every one will have a consequence. The consequence will depend upon how you value life and opportunity. There are no shortcuts to success. As in Mark's case, he got a second chance, but then he did not use it and life continued to be difficult for him.

Ryan Hershman

Fathers not only tell us how to live-they show us.

I often went down to the middle school during their wrestling season, to see how the future looked for my team. One year, I saw this little boy that always had a great "game face" on before his match. You can tell a lot about a boy by the way he looks before stepping out on the mat. There is no place to hide and you can't blame anyone but yourself if things don't go right. This is one of the reasons so many young kids don't want to wrestle. The risk of embarrassing yourself in front of your friends and family is too great.

Ryan always tried his hardest and loved it when his sister and mother were in the stands. They were great cheerleaders for Ryan. This is another thing about wrestling that sets it apart from most sports. There are so many people telling you what to do, that it can get confusing. Even your Grandmother, who doesn't know anything about the sport, can yell out instructions.

I noticed that one person was usually missing from his matches, and that was Ryan's dad. I started encouraging Ryan throughout the season and we became very close. By the time Ryan was in high school, he was *hooked* on being a champion wrestler. Ryan made it to the County Championship finals, when his Mom came to speak to me. She and Ryan's father were divorced now, but she shared with me that Ryan's dad was in critical condition at the hospital and had overdosed on drugs earlier in the day. She wanted Ryan to be focused on winning the championships and asked us not to say anything until after the finals.

Ryan won his final match and jumped into my brother's arms. It was a moment that sticks in your mind like it was yesterday. With tears of happiness coming down his Mom's face, she hugged Ryan and walked him out of the gym, to give him the bad news. My wife and I met the family at the hospital after the tournament. Ryan was so proud of his gold medal, that he put it around his dad's neck in the hospital room.

The following Christmas, I get a phone call from Ryan's mom. The father was going crazy, breaking into her apartment, trying to hurt the family. She asked if I could come and get Ryan and keep him at my house for the next couple of days until things calmed down. I was happy to help and get Ryan out of the situation.

The next two years were very tough for Ryan. He tried many different sports but never achieved the same kind of success he had as a freshman wrestler. Instead of working hard at one or two sports, Ryan changed his lifestyle. The people he hung around with were not athletes and lived with different priorities. By the time Ryan was a senior, his self-esteem was way down and his future was bleak.

His life was filled with drugs and I would never hear from him. That is one thing that seems to be a pattern. When things are going well with my former wrestlers, I always hear from them. But if they are doing bad things that would disappoint me, they hide. They know how the importance of living a good lifestyle is with me. So instead of facing me, they would rather hide.

I would hear from Ryan every couple of years. When he did call, I would take him to church with my family. We would eat dinner together and talk about changing his ways. He was surrounding himself with such bad kids, that he didn't have much of a chance for success. Ryan is now meeting us at church on Sunday evenings with his wife. His struggles with drugs continue but he enjoys going to our church. I have faith that the Lord has a special plan for Ryan. I look forward to the future and the many people that will learn from Ryan's past.

Ryan's story reminds me of the unique and crucial role fathers have in the lives of their children. It's not enough just to be present. Dads must be actively involved and a vigorously interested participant in the child rearing process. A Christ-like example is the greatest gift parents can give their children.

John Durso

When evil desire demands to be fed, we must say no.

When you lead a good lifestyle, you don't have to look over your shoulder worrying if you did something wrong. It's a great feeling to have. One day, I got a call over the school's PA system, saying to come to the front office. The principal met me there with a sad look on her face. She took me into her office and sat me down. I was told that one of my former wrestlers, John Durso, was in a bad car accident in Colorado and it didn't look like he was going to make it.

I immediately went to the back of my school and started praying, asking God for some help. John was attending college in Boulder and living the normal fraternity lifestyle. Being only

19-years-old didn't stop John from getting alcohol at the local restaurant. He was always the "life of the party" in high school, but now his drinking was getting dangerous. One night, John and his friend drank three bottles of whisky before they decided to do some "off road" driving. John brought a 22- caliber rifle with them and took off his seatbelt to shoot out a road sign. Traveling at 70 mph, John's friend was unable to control the truck around a sharp curve. Sliding off the road, their truck hit the side of a mountain and flipped over. The paramedics needed the 'Jaws of Life' to get the boys out of the car. John had lacerations on his brain and was not breathing at the time. When his parents flew in from San Diego, John was still in a coma. The doctors told them their son had a slim chance of surviving.

Thoughts of John in his high school days went through my mind. He had very supportive parents and always had a smile on his face. John was friends with everyone and just loved having a good time. After 11 days in intensive care, John was able to come home to San Diego for 2 months of daily rehabilitation. When he came home for rehabilitation, our wrestling team was outside of his house waiting. He was able to recognize us, but his smile was not the same. God answered my prayers, as He likes to do, and saved John.

With time and lots of therapy, John was able to go back to Boulder and graduate. He learned that he could go to college and still have fun without alcohol. He washed dishes in a sorority house and would tell us stories of how alcohol changed the girls. He lives home now and is back to his normal self. John has just celebrated his third year living alcohol free. He helps out with our wrestling team and always speaks about the dangers of alcohol. He has learned from his mistakes and is not afraid to tell others how his poor choices caused problems for not only him but also his family.

Respect is a big quality missing in young people today. Respect for other people, respect for property, respect for the law and most importantly respect for your own bodies. We have to learn to take care of our bodies. It is the most important possession you have. The Bible says to treat your body like a temple . . . not the temple of doom. The consequences are so positive when you take care of your body.

Thrifty Drugs

We stumble over pebbles not mountains.

In my second year at Mt. Carmel, I had a different type of seniors. They were used to following and not leading by example. The previous senior class were poor role models. They were very hard workers in practice, but led bad lifestyles off the mats. They won many matches, but when it came to the things they really wanted . . . it never happened. This experience helped me design my "Formula for a Blessed Life." This class of seniors did not have good examples to follow and it hurt them in the end.

To change things up one day, I decided to take the team on a long run. Thrifty Drug store had a deal on ice cream. You could get a cone with two scoops for only 49 cents! You could choose from15 different flavors, so that was something this ice cream "freak" couldn't pass up.

I got the whole team lined up and one after another; they got their favorite cone. The seniors went first, and then went outside to eat their ice cream. With only two sophomore wrestlers left in the line, I heard a tap on the window. I looked outside and there were my two captains, smiling at me, drinking a bottle of Gatorade. I knew they didn't bring any money with them because the run was a surprise. They must have stolen the Gatorade!

I looked at the last two sophomores in line and said to them, "I want you to watch what happens to our captains this Saturday at the county championships." The goal of most of our wrestlers is to qualify for the state meet. Sure enough both senior captains got beat. The crazy thing was those two sophomores surprised everybody and qualified. It was a lesson those boys would never forget.

What kind of lifestyle do you believe in and live? Is it one of focused selfishness or one of lovingly seeking to meet the needs of others? God is always with us, wanting us to be content, no matter what the circumstances are.

Bachelor Party

One little word can spare us a lot of trouble. It's NO.

The only other Christian in my family is my sister, Jackie. She lives with her family around the Portland, Oregon area. One summer, I decided to take my girls up there for a visit. We had a dog and cat, so I asked a former wrestler of mine to "house sit" for us. The trip was going fine, but I missed being away from San Diego. We decided to cut our vacation a couple of days short and head home.

Portland is usually a two-day drive but coming from New York, speed limits are optional. When we got to the half way point, I looked at Stacey and asked, "Would you like to sleep in your own bed tonight?" A smile on her face said, yes. I told her to sit back and take a nap because I was going to "power drive."

After 18 hours behind the wheel, I finally turned down our block. Something seemed unusual because there was 20 cars parked outside my house and all lights were turned off. I got out of the van and told my wife that I was going to check things out. As I got closer to my house, I heard music and laughing coming from inside. I "tip-toed" to the back yard and saw ex-wrestlers coming out of the garage with cups of beer. Getting a closer look through the windows, I saw kids sitting in our living room. They all had flashlights and were sitting in a big circle.

My jaw dropped when I saw the two naked girls dancing

in the middle of the circle. I had to go out front and tell my wife that the boys were having a bachelor party. I was expecting Stacey to go crazy, but she reacted just the opposite. She said, "Let the boys have their fun. We will go to our friend's house and ask if we can sleep on their couch." Can you imagine, driving 18 hours to find out that your ex-wrestlers were using your house for a bachelor party?

We got to my friend's house and woke them. They agreed to play along with a quickly hashed plan and let me use the phone. I tried to call my house and see if the wrestlers would pick up. They were not that dumb and wouldn't answer the phone. Finally at 3 in the morning, they answered. I told them that we were changing our plans and would arrive the next morning at 8 A.M. They were surprised but said they would be expecting us.

I didn't arrive until 10 A.M., hoping that the house would be clean. The first place I went was the garage, seeing if there were any remnants of the keg of beer. The only thing left was the plastic cap that goes on the keg, advertising the type of beer in it. There was that distinct smell of spilled beer on our carpets, but I didn't say anything about it.

A couple of weeks later at the wedding. Stacey and I asked all of the former wrestlers if we could get a picture together. They thought it was a great idea and we walked to a quieter room. As I situated the wrestlers and got my camera out, I reached in my back pocket. I brought out a pair of Stacey's underpants and asked the wrestlers, "Do you guys know where these came from? My wife found them and wants to know who they belong to?"

Their jaws dropped as I clicked away at the camera. I then told them that we hadn't come home on Saturday morning but on Friday evening. "We saw what you were doing in our house with the strippers." I continued clicking pictures as their faces turned red.

They all started laughing when they realized we weren't

that mad. However, I was hurt by their lack of sorrow. They took my house for granted and took advantage of my trust without any remorse. This is one of the problems our youth have today—a lack of concern for the consequences of their actions. I guess the moral is to choose your house sitters wisely.

In Summary: CHARACTER COUNTS

Reputation is what others think you are but character is what you *really* are. Being successful takes character. Many people today will do "whatever it takes" to achieve success. My approach is just the opposite. By working hard and doing the right thing all the time, God will reward you. You might not win the championship, but knowing you did it the right way will stay with you forever.

Loyalty

I am a firm believer in loyalty. In today's society, the question is, "What have you done for me lately?" Loyalty today shifts as often as the wind. Young people must be taught the importance of being loyal to friends and family, remaining loyal to your word, loyal to a team, loyal to a task or goal.

The Power Of Words

A word of encouragement can make the difference between giving up and going on. All of us need a word of encouragement from time to time, especially when we are facing a new challenge. But we also need words of appreciation and commendation as we carry out our daily responsibilities. Many people crave some small sign of approval. Every word we say on earth is heard in heaven. Use your words to strengthen and encourage one another.

We have a tendency to embellish the truth in order to impress people. If we place our faith in the Lord, lying is inconsistent with what God expects us to be. Honesty means never having to look over your shoulder. One of the main problems with society today is the lack of honesty. Even our leaders, those who hold the highest political positions, often misrepresent the truth or blatantly lie. With honesty comes trust. Are you known as an honest person? There is such a feeling of self worth when your friends know they can trust you because of your honesty. Becoming one who is known to be truthful will only serve your future well.

Giving

Giving is a true measure of love. There are many people around us who are poor. Even though we can't solve their problems, we can show them that we care. We can treat them with courtesy and respect. We can pray for them or write them letters of encouragement. It only takes a moment to be kind, but the result can last forever. God is more concerned with *why* we give than how *much* we give. God is the ultimate giver. You don't always need materials things to give; sometimes the greatest gift is our time. Because God gives us all we need, let's give to others in their need. The greatest blessings come to the one who freely gives and expects nothing in return.

Respect

One of the big qualities missing in young people today is respect. Respect for other people, respect for property, respect for the law, their country and most importantly, for their own bodies. Drugs, alcohol, tattoos, piercing and a total disregard for fitness are seen in our youth. Take care of yourself! It is the most important possession you have. Remember what I mentioned earlier, your body is a temple of God and not the "temple of doom". Make exercise something you do for the rest of your life. The consequences are so positive when you take care of yourself.

PART THREE
A Blessed Life

Chapter Nine

SALVATION
God's Plan for Your Life

By now, you have heard the simple formula and read many stories about: **Dedication, Education, Affiliation and Living a Good Life Style.** It is a simple formula, once you look at it. You have heard about the importance of working hard. I am sure many people have spoken with you about reaching your goals through hard work. Living a good lifestyle might be a little different for many people. The message that kids get from watching most of the television shows today is one far removed from the good lifestyle God expects of us. Then throw in the peer pressure and most kids fall short when trouble begins. So let's talk about the bottom line. What do you have to gain by following this formula? The final answer to the formula is, **a Blessed Life.** You might ask, "What does a blessed life look like?"

Before I answer that question, I must ask another. Do you have everything you ever wanted? Whenever I speak to a group, I look at them with my hands raised and say, "I can honestly say that now I have everything I ever wanted." I never had that much growing up, especially with six kids on a teacher's salary. I just wanted a family that I could love and take care of. I wanted a job that I looked forward to everyday. Lastly, I wanted a house I could call home and share with my friends. God answered all of my prayers and gave me everything I ever wanted. I was taught that God wants us to ask for *specific* things. The Bible says that all good things come from God. When He answers our prayers,

He wants us to tell others about Him. God wants to bless you and me.

How do you have a blessed life? First, comes a relationship with our Lord and Savior, Jesus Christ. When God becomes the "head coach" of your life, you will find out. He has a plan for your life. Not just any old plan, but a **perfect** plan. *God may conceal the purpose of his ways; but His ways are not without purpose.* When we live according to God's design, we will be successful in carrying out His plan for our lives. My pastor makes it even easier by saying that all one has to do is "obey God."

Having a blessed life will help you get through the tough times in your life. If there is one thing I can guarantee for everyone is that you *will* suffer through hard times. God never promised that once you become a Christian, your life would be easy. But what He does promise is to never leave you or forsake you.

For the Christian, the real reward for following Christ is heaven, the endless life and joy with Jesus. Funerals are no fun. Death and separation is painful, but as Christians, we don't grieve as those with no hope. We can rejoice, even with tears, because our loved one has taken up a new residence in heaven. When a Christian dies, he has just begun to live. The hope of heaven is yours no matter your age, condition or circumstances. If you are a Christian, the hope of heaven is yours. Life in that celestial city will be wonderful. No more death, sorrow, mourning or pain. God will make all things new. Are you sure you are on your way to heaven? 87% of people *think* they are going to heaven. To get to that golden city, you have to admit your sin and trust in Jesus Christ as the One who died to pay the penalty for your sins on the cross. We still grieve when a believing loved one dies. Grief is love's expression. But beneath it all is an unshakable joy; because we know our loved one is in heaven.

My mom told me the story of her dad's passing. He didn't leave much to the family, but still, my uncles fought over the inheritance. This made me ask my Dad about his will.

The last thing I want is for my brothers and sisters to fight over the inheritance Dad leaves us. Money will not change my life, except for the worse. Man-made wills can fail, but there is no ambiguous language about the inheritance God has in store for us. The inheritance for the Christian is heaven and it is guaranteed forever.

I don't remember too much about my grandfather. We lived far away from him and only visited on holidays, but I won't forget him saying, "Don't cry for me after I am gone." My grandfather knew that Jesus is preparing a place for us and preparing us for that place. Nothing on earth can compare to being with Christ in heaven.

As a new Christian, I began hearing that God had a plan for my life. It is not any old plan, but a **perfect** plan. Now that I look back at the trials of West Point, I realize that even that time of my life, helped prepare my testimony. The wife and the job I have was all part of God's plan. Again, *God may conceal the purpose of his ways, but His ways are not without purpose.* The Lord wants to use you more then you ever thought possible. God uses *ordinary* people to carry out His *extraordinary* plan. The Lord intervenes and saves broken lives today, but He does this by mainly using us. God will send you to help Him mend broken lives.

In times past, I would take pride in my wrestling team's successes and begin to think that I didn't need His help. He allowed me to fail, so He could teach me that true success comes through His grace. God helps those who know they are helpless.

Following the 2004 wrestling season, I fell into a deep depression. Our team had its best chance ever to finally win the championship. I thought if we won, I would get the recognition earned for the 26 years of coaching I had put in. I always knew I was a good coach, doing the right things for kids. But without that banner hanging in the gym, I was just another coach. The problem was that I was relying on unreliable kids, or so I thought. I prayed and asked God to show me what I should do. The very next day, an announcement came saying our school would have to lose a science teacher because of financial cutbacks. That one teacher happened to be the only state wrestling champ our school had ever produced. If I stepped down as head coach, the science teacher's job would be saved. I thanked God the whole time I was writing the letter of resignation. So, I willingly became an assistant coach, concentrating on building relationships with kids. God rewarded our team with its first ever championship team.

My last year being the head coach was difficult because all I wanted to do was win the championship title. *I forgot that the world crowns success but God crowns faithfulness.* Many times in our lives, no one acknowledges our efforts. As a wrestling coach, I had to put in countless hours behind the scenes. If you expect people to appreciate that, you will be disappointed. Don't be discouraged and never give up. God sees and knows everything you are doing. What you do will have eternal significance in God's eyes. You are never in the wrong place to serve God. When we live according to God's design, we will be successful in carrying out His plan for our lives.

People fail to see the need for salvation by looking at others and saying, "I'm not as bad as him." Romans 3:23 says, "We have all sinned and fallen short of God's glory." Our salvation depends on what Christ did for us. Our rewards depend on how we live for Him. For years West Point was a thorn in my side. If anything went wrong it was West Point's fault. It was my dirty little secret that I only shared with my closest friends. The fear of what people might think of me if they knew the real truth haunted me. The only way I could enjoy the future was to accept God's forgiveness of my past. No problem or crisis is so big that it baffles God's wisdom and power.

When life is peaceful, people are self-sufficient. But when the going gets rough, they are swept off their feet. Because they have refused God's help, they have nothing to hold on to and are easily overwhelmed. People who cling to the Lord have someone to rely on in every circumstance of life. *God has not promised to keep us from life's storms, but to keep us through them.*

Chapter Ten

STORIES OF FORGIVENESS, RESTORATION, AND FINDING A PURPOSE

A Return To West Point

*To enjoy the future, you must accept
God's forgiveness for the past.*

One summer, my high school class was celebrating our 30th reunion. I thought it would be a great time to bring my family back to New York and show them where I grew up. We drove upstate to the little town, where I spent the first nine years of my life. The town is run down now, but the people are the nicest you could ever meet and they love my dad. On our trip back down to Long Island, I decided to stop and show my family West Point. My wife was impressed with the beauty and history of the place. While visiting there I was hoping to contact three people. One was an incoming freshman, which I knew I didn't have much of a chance to see. The second was a recent West Point graduate who had attended my high school and was working near by. The third was a man named Lieutenant Colonel Greg Daniels. Greg was the "huddle leader" for the West Point Fellowship of Christian Athletes club. I had never met Greg, but God was telling me to look him up.

Our first stop was, of course, the wrestling room. It was

in an old building where, in my days at West Point, the freshman dances were held. On the walls, outside the room, were the pictures of the past Army wrestling teams. As my family and I looked at the pictures, many familiar faces popped up. The most prominent faces were of the guys that wrestled for my dad, including my older brother, Mike. When my daughters asked, "Daddy, why isn't your picture up there?" I faced the hardest part of the whole day. It was a very humbling experience, but I had to tell them that their daddy was a "knucklehead" back then. I had to explain, "I had made some bad choices in my life and while I was attending West Point I was caught cheating. Because of my cheating, I was kicked out of West Point." Admitting my mistakes to my daughters was very hard to do because it was forcing me to face a period of my life that I had left hidden for so very long.

Our next stop was to find Colonel Daniels. My hopes of finding him were pretty slim. Due to the 9/11 situations, the security around West Point had been re-enforced. As we walked toward the Physical Education Department, which was off-limits to civilian people, a lady soldier passed us. I stopped her and asked if she could tell us where to find Colonel Daniels' office. Her answer surprised me. She responded with, "Yes, I am going to see him now and I will get you by the security." When God has you on a mission, there will be no doors that stop you.

Meeting Colonel Daniels was a great reward. His first question was to know if I had ever been to West Point before. When I shared with him that I had attended West Point but had been involved in the 1976 cheating scandal, he replied, "Wow, the BIG one!" It was at that point that I shared with Greg my desire to one day return and give my testimony to the cadets of West Point. Although I had given my testimony many times to people on the West Coast, I felt very convicted to share it with people who could better understand the West Point experience. Who better than the people of West Point? Colonel Daniels told me that the Fellowship of Christian Athletes had an annual breakfast for the whole "post" and he would think about giving me an opportunity to speak during the event. As my family and I walked out of his office, I knew it was God's plan for us to be there. God's plan for me to speak at West Point came through in the fall of 2003. The really wild part was, not only did West Point ask me to speak, but they also paid me to do it!

For 27 years, West Point was the place of my biggest failure, something I wanted to forget. Now, through the grace of God, I was returning to the site of much pain and distress, to share how God used the experience to mold me into the man I am. That cold October weekend was one of the greatest weekends of my life. Instead of being treated as "the cheater", I was treated with respect and dignity. I spoke to the wrestling team, the football coaches and finally the cadets. I had asked for God's forgiveness a long time ago and this was an opportunity to ask West Point to forgive me. As a parting gift, the Commandant of Cadets gave me a medallion and a West Point shirt. He asked that I wear it with pride, knowing how difficult it was to finally come back and share my story.

Evil can hang a shroud of despair over any word or experience in our lives. It may be the name of a person who has deeply hurt you, or, in my situation, a place where I failed. It is through the grace of God that those events can be redefined by the dynamic power of God's love.

Joe Tezak

Even in the darkest hours, Christians have the brightest hope.

One summer, I got a phone call from a man. He told me his son was visiting from England, where he lived with his mom. He asked if his son could workout with our wrestling team. I quickly agreed and came to know Joe Tezak. Joe had so much fun with our team that he called up his mom and said he wanted to stay in San Diego to wrestle for us. I'll never forget, we had a surf contest for all of the wrestlers and the only one who showed up on our whole team was Joe. So I made him the winner of the surf contest. Joe was not blessed with the most athletic ability, but made up for it by working extremely hard.

He loved wrestling and that's what set him apart from most other kids. Joe was very popular at our school and was voted Homecoming King his senior year. He qualified for the state wrestling championships, but never placed at the tournament. Being a 103-pound wrestler, most colleges didn't recruit him, especially since the lightest weight class in college was 118 pounds. But Joe's desire to wrestle in college took him to our Counseling Center to look for any small colleges that offered wrestling. He found some very small schools around the country that were interested and he contacted all the coaches.

I remember Joe coming back from a recruiting trip in North Dakota. He visited a small school in Bismarck named the University of Mary. It was cold and far away, but as soon as he met the coach, Milo Trustee, he knew Mary was the place for him.

In Joe's freshmen year, his dad came down with cancer. I got a phone call telling me that if I wanted to see Mr. Tezak before he died, I'd better rush to the hospital. I had never met a person on their "death bed" before. What do you say to a man who's living his last few moments on earth? It was very, very hard. Stacey and I walked into the hospital room and saw Joe's dad and I began to cry, thanking him for all the things he had done for my family and me. As Joe's dad held my hand, I asked him what I could do to help.

Mr. Tezak looked at me and said, "Coach, you are closer to my son than anyone else here. Please, look after my son."

I said, "Okay, Mr. Tezak. I'm going to treat Joe like he's my son."

The next day, Mr. Tezak passed away.

That year, Joe qualified for the NAIA nationals. Knowing if his Dad were alive, he would have flown out to watch him wrestle, I got on an airplane and flew to beautiful Butte, Montana for the NAIA National Championships. It was so funny, because I told Joe that I was not going to be able to make it. I was trying to surprise him by not telling the truth. But when I walked into the arena in Butte, Joe acted like he knew I was coming and just said, "Hey, Coach."

Joe's first match was against a wrestler who only had one leg. I thought for sure we had a great chance to win that match. But the guy used his disability to his advantage and he pinned Joe. When Joe was wrestling back, he won his next match and then had a guy whose last name was Fish. In wrestling terminology, anyone called "fish" is usually a very bad wrestler. So I thought to myself, *There's no way we're going to lose to a guy named Fish.* Sure enough, Joe lost and was out of the tournament.

At the end of the tournament, they had a party for all the wrestlers on Joe's team. Milo Trustee was a fantastic man and mentor for Joe, especially after losing his father. We were all very appreciative of that. I constantly asked Joe to come home for the summers so I could see him growing into a man. I could only imagine how hard it was not having a dad around.

During the next two years I attended the NAIA tournament in beautiful Jamestown, North Dakota. Joe was an All American both years. As a junior, he made it to the finals, but lost a very close match. We were all very heart broken for him.

Joe's senior year came around and his NAIA tournament was the same weekend as my state-wrestling tournament. Not being able to watch him wrestle was like telling Joe, "You're a man now, Joe. You're out there on your own." Joe's tournament was on a Thursday and Friday, where our tournament was Friday and Saturday. I can remember being in our hotel room on that Friday night when my wife, Stacey called. She said, "Congratulations! You have your first national champion. Joey beat the same guy that beat him the year before to win the NAIA National Championships!"

Everyone in our hotel room was crying with happiness. Right before our finals started, Sandy Stevens announced to the crowd of 6,000, "California has a National Champion and his name is Joe Tezak." I can't tell you the amount of pride I had for my "step-son." It still brings tears to my eyes.

Joe wanted to be a teacher, so he came back to Mount Carmel. His goal was to teach and coach wrestling at his old high school. I was so excited and was able to have him student teach at our school. It was the year to have my teaching evaluated and the principal was doing the evaluation. In our meeting before the year started, the principal asked me if there was anything he could do to help me out. I asked him to critique Joe, as a teacher, and give him an honest chance to get hired.

Joe was doing a great job in the classroom and the students really looked up to him. He was assigned to an experienced teacher at Mt. Carmel, one who would monitor his daily routine. That person is called a Master Teacher and his evaluation is very important. The teacher would come in and talk to me about how Joe was doing. Joe took his student teaching very seriously and worked very hard at it, but our principal never went in to observe him. It wasn't until the last day of school, right before final exams, that the principal actually went in and watched Joe teach. I'll never forget, because his Master Teacher came walking through my locker room and said to me, "Hey! The principal was in the room watching Joe teach, and Joe did a good job." I was excited, because I knew there was a teaching opening at our school in Joe's area for the upcoming year.

I went and spoke to the principal and he had a totally different evaluation. Watching Joe teach for only fifteen minutes, the principal told me that Joe would never be anything more than just an "average" teacher. He said Joe "wasn't good enough" to come back to his own school and be a teacher. I was so disappointed in the principal. I know, as a Christian, you're supposed to forgive, but I had a difficult time forgiving him, and I certainly have not been able to forget.

That summer, Joe was in San Diego and he knew our wrestling team was entering a tournament in Hawaii the next year. Joe formed his own moving company to help other boys raise money for the trip. He must have moved six or seven families with the help of some wrestlers. Joe didn't take any money for himself. He divided up all the proceeds to the wrestlers that helped do the move.

In the fall, Joe went back to the University of Mary to start his Master's degree. That Christmas, our team flew to Hawaii for a wrestling tournament, while Joe was stuck in Bismarck, North Dakota. We had to fly into Los Angeles and take a school bus, two hours back to San Diego. It was a long trip and I didn't get to bed until 5:30 in the morning.

At 7:00 A.M., the phone rang. It was Joe's mom, telling me there had been a terrible accident on New Year's Eve. Joe was at a party with a bunch of his wrestling friends. The party was in a hotel room and the boys were messing around with a Murphy bed (a hide-a-bed used in many hotels). When Joe laid down on the edge of the bed, one of his friends picked up the Murphy bed and closed Joe in it. Joe's head hit the wall and his body slid down. When they pulled the bed down, Joe was hurt and told everyone he couldn't move his arms or legs. He knew something was terribly wrong.

The college kids at the party called the paramedics. When they arrived, the paramedics thought that it was just a bunch of drunken college kids pulling a prank. Soon after arriving, the paramedics walked back out of the hotel. Luckily, some of the girls at the party were actually nursing students. They went running outside to tell the paramedics that Joe was indeed really hurt. When the paramedics returned they looked at Joe and said, "This is going to be the most expensive taxi ride you ever had. Are you sure you need us, it will cost you $500." Joe claimed that he knew he was hurt and that he couldn't move his legs.

The paramedics did not follow the normal procedure for a neck injury. Instead of using a backboard and neck brace, they picked Joe up by grabbing the sheets from the bed. In fact, one of the paramedics' hands slipped and Joe fell to the floor. They picked him up and put him on the gurney for the trip to the hospital.

In their initial report, the paramedics wrote that Joe *could* move his arms and his legs. Upon arrival to the hospital, the attending physician examined Joe and wrote down that he could not move his arms or legs. That tells you something went wrong between the hotel room and the trip to the hospital that caused Joe to be paralyzed. What that also means was a million dollar lawsuit. To top it all off, Joe did not have any medical insurance.

After I received the initial phone call, I went directly to the airport and got on the next flight to Bismarck. Thoughts went through my mind, "What could I possibly say to this boy?" I promised his dad I would take care of his son. Now I have to walk into a hospital room and try to tell a 24 year old that everything was going to be okay when I didn't know what the future held for him. I believe that God has a plan for our lives, but how do you explain that to a boy who has just been paralyzed? It was probably one of the hardest things that I ever had to do.

I met his step-mom at the airport and she told me that I had to be strong in front of Joe. I am an emotional Spaniard and I knew it would very hard to do. In a way, I felt guilty. I felt I should have taken Joe to Hawaii with our wrestling team, especially since he helped raise so much money with his moving company. I walked in the hospital room and saw Joe lying in the bed. His strong, six-pack stomach muscles were replaced by a rounded belly, like many paralyzed people begin to develop. Joe just looked and me and said, "Hey, Coach."

Instead of feeling sorry for himself, or being mad at whoever picked up the bed, Joe was always positive. I stayed three days with Joe, spending time trying to see what was happening, and never once was Joe negative. The day before I left, I walked in and tried to say good-bye to Joe and had a hard time holding back the tears. I cried and told him that I loved him and wanted him to come back to California so we could take care of him.

As mentioned before the hard part was Joe didn't have any insurance. His grandparents lived in Denver, close to a hospital well-known for treating spinal injuries. Because of Joe's lack of insurance, he had to stay in Bismarck. I questioned how many people did they have to work with in Bismarck that were in the same medical condition as Joe. As I flew back to San Diego, I had a very helpless feeling. I felt that I had failed Joe's dad.

Joe started physical therapy and rehab in Bismarck. He applied for a scholarship to the "Miami Project", a spinal cord rehab center in Miami. Former professional football player for the Miami Dolphins, Nick Bouniconti, started the center when his son, Mark was paralyzed in a football accident. Joe was in Miami for two years going through therapy.

This was about the same time my Mom passed away. Then, my Dad, who lived in Florida at that time, fell into a deep depression. On spring break, I flew out to Florida to see my dad and visit Joe at the same time. Dad and I drove down to Miami to see Joe together. We saw his apartment and the hospital where Joe went for rehab. It was amazing to see how Joe was able to get around.

I'll never forget going into his apartment and not seeing any food in the refrigerator. We put Joe right in the car and went to the grocery store. We bought as much food as we could fit in his apartment. The Gov was in a depression, but after seeing Joe and what he had to go through, it was amazing how my Dad instantly felt a little bit better.

Since Joe didn't have any insurance, we decided to help by setting up some fundraising events. With the help of many people in San Diego, we were able to have two different dinners and help raise money for Joe.

Suddenly, Joe didn't want to be a teacher anymore. After his two years in Miami, Joe returned to Bismarck and got his Master's Degree. A wrestler's dad from our high school was able to get Joe a job with U.S. Customs Agency. Joe is still helping out our wrestling team, coaching on the edge of the mat in his wheelchair.

Many times our wrestling team will go to a lake that has a jogging path around it. Joe will get in his specialized racing wheel chair and put the wrestlers through a series of exercises at every mile marker. It is amazing the lessons that Joe has taught us, especially with his positive outlook, in this difficult situation.

My daughters love it when Joe comes over. They get in his chair and wheel around our house. It's amazing that, sometimes when we think we have it bad, we think of Joe and he inspires us all.

The Challenged Athletes Foundation has been a big part of Joe's recovery. They awarded Joe money to buy a racing wheel chair and a hand cycle. They raise money by having a triathlon once a year in La Jolla, California. Because of the money they made available to Joe, I felt an obligation to help them raise money. At forty-five years old, I went into their half ironman triathlon. After swimming 1.2 miles in the ocean, I hear the announcer say, "There goes Robin Williams off on the bike!"

The actor, Robin Williams is a big supporter of The Challenged Athletes Foundation. As I'm getting on my bike, I said to myself, "Well, I think I'm going to ride my bike with Robin Williams." You see, Robin Williams was a high school wrestler. Even though he was guarded by a bunch of professional cyclists, I would follow him closely. Whenever I had a chance, I would swerve in between the professional cyclists, ride up and talk to Robin. He told me how injuries cut short his wrestling career.

After I got off the bike, my whole wrestling team was waiting for me to run the half marathon. We ended up running the half marathon for Joe. Now he helps the Challenged Athletes Foundation by personal appearances. Joe tells about the strength from the Lord given to him, especially when things get tough. It has just been a blessing for Joe and my family. Is there a problem too big for you to handle? Put your hand in the Lord's.

No problem or crisis is so big that it baffles God's wisdom. Because He cares for us, we are invited to tell Him about any and all of our concerns. (1 Peter 5:7)

Long Beach Jordan

Dare to give your hassles and heartaches a more challenging name, such as "growing pains," with an emphasis on growing.

Ever since I was a young boy, "sucked out" during Christmas time, I would watch the Rose Bowl. I would see the USC cheerleaders, all pretty, dancing on TV in the sunshine. I would be thinking, "Man! I've got to get out to California!" On my first trip out to California, it was beautiful—warm weather and palm trees all over the place. It was the place I had to go. I interviewed at a high school in Long Beach and eventually got the job. I was living in Hermosa Beach, one of the most beautiful beaches in the world. I had a teaching job and was living with my older brother. What could be better then that?

I started coaching the wrestling team at Long Beach Jordan High School. They hadn't had a team for two years. We practiced for three weeks trying to get ready, not knowing exactly what kind of competition we had.

Our first competition was called call "a five-way." We went to a high school and wrestled four different teams in one day. In Florida, I had a very good team. I used an incentive to get my wrestlers to pin their opponents. If they pinned 3 wrestlers in a row, I would buy them a milkshake. But if they got pinned, they would owe me a milkshake. I almost went broke that year from buying milkshakes. With my new team, since they had not wrestled before, I told them if they pinned two guys in a row, I would buy them a milkshake. But if they got pinned once, they would owe me

On the first match of the day, my little 103-pound wrestler goes out on the mat. During the first couple of minutes of the match, my wrestler bites his opponent right in the neck. His opponent starts screaming and the coach from the other team comes running across the mat. He sees the bite mark and starts cursing at me. "What kind of coach teaches his kids to bite people?" I'm looking at the other coach saying, "Sorry, but I've never coached these kids before. This is their first competition. I'd never teach them that."

During that match, one of my JV kids is sitting in the stands. He has a "walkman" on and thought it would be funny to make up a rumor. He starts telling everyone in the stands that the President of the United Sates had just been assassinated. All the mothers in the stands start crying, thinking that our President had been assassinated. The president at the time was Ronald Reagan and he was from California. So everyone in the gym thinks that Ronald Reagan has just been assassinated.

That wasn't the worst part of the day. At the end of the day, they are ready to hand out the awards. Of course, since my whole team stunk, they were on the bus waiting to leave. I went over to thank the coach for inviting us to his tournament and he says to me, "We would like to hand out the awards, but someone has stolen the microphone. People said they saw your team around the microphone. Do you think you could ask your team if someone has it?"

Of course, I'm very embarrassed and sad. I go walking out to the parking lot where our team bus was parked. I see the bus rocking up and down. My kids are laughing and joking and dancing on the bus. I walk on the bus and asked everyone to sit down and be quiet. I tell them that the microphone in the gym is missing. "No one is going to get in trouble, but if you have the microphone, I'm not even going to look. Could you please pass the microphone up to the front?"

I put my hand inside the bus with my head turned away. One of the first times in a long time, I prayed to God, "Please,

God! Don't let that microphone come down. Please, God!" Then, thump! There's the microphone in my hand.

I have to go walking back into the gym and give the coach his microphone. The coach is standing in front of the crowd, yelling at the top of his voice without a microphone, "In third place, at 103 pounds . . ."

I slowly walked across the gym, in front of everyone, with the microphone in my hands saying, "Sorry, Coach."

I walk out to the bus, and the kids, not thinking that they did anything wrong, are still jumping up and down. Remember that milkshake deal that I told you about? Well, that day, my wrestling team owed me 38 milkshakes!

I only lasted one year at Jordan High School. As a coach, I was accustomed to winning. The losing made me re-think the idea of coaching high school wrestling. On the other hand, we often take pride in our successes and begin to think we don't need the Lord's help. He will allow us to fail, so He can teach us that true success comes through His grace. God helps those who know they are helpless. I moved to San Diego, not knowing what God in store for me.

Don Rohn

In the dreams of life, God is the director behind the scenes.

In high school, I didn't have many girlfriends. Either I was afraid of them or my Dad would encourage me to stay away from them. Right at the end of my senior year, I started dating one of my sister's best friends. One of the benefits of having a younger sister was that she always had her girlfriends over at the house. So I got to date a couple of them.

This girl was just like my sister. She was a great girl and knew everything about me. When I went to West Point, I discovered that having a girlfriend back home meant everything. Just getting a letter in the mail was something that everyone lived for.

I would get letters from the girl and she would come and visit me, whenever I was out of confinement. She went to college in western Pennsylvania, known for its great wrestling team.

Of course, I always wanted to know about all the great wrestlers from Clarion. It was funny because the Clarion wrestling coach, Bob Bubb, was a strong Christian, and many of the kids who wrestled for Coach Bubb became Christians.

I remember one time, the girl told me on the phone that she had been "saved" and I kind of laughed at her. I didn't really know what that meant. We dated on and off for about three years, and after I left West Point and I went to Southern Connecticut State College. Having Spring Break at a regular college was something new to me.

All my friends at Southern Connecticut were going to celebrate spring break down in Daytona Beach. They were making the long drive down to Florida, but I wanted to go see my girlfriend in western Pennsylvania. A friend and I hitchhiked thirteen and a half hours across the state of Pennsylvania, one of the most boring states there is. It was cold and the only people giving us rides were truckers. We ended up pulling into Clarion, at 3:30 in the morning.

I knocked on my girlfriend's door and expected her to be very happy to see me. She wasn't that thrilled. I couldn't understand it. She tried to make the excuse that it was 3:00 in the morning, and she couldn't be that happy at that hour. I had to remind her that I had just hitchhiked over thirteen hours to come and see her. I could tell something was wrong—something I didn't know about. The next day when she was showing me around campus, she wouldn't even hold my hand.

One of the National Champions from Clarion was named Don Rohn. When I would ask about him, she would tell me that he was a ladies man. If you didn't go to bed with him, he didn't want to know you. He sounded like a great guy, because I knew *my* girlfriend wasn't sleeping with him. I didn't have to worry about him stealing her away. After spending one day at Clarion and feeling as though I was intruding, I got on a bus and left for upstate New York to visit my uncle and friend at another college.

I returned home later in the week and a received a letter from the girl. It was a "Dear John Letter", telling me that for her birthday present, she became engaged to Don Rohn. Don had had an accident and one of his fingers was amputated. The girl used to visit him in the hospital all the time, and of course he realized how nice the girl was. They ended up getting engaged and have been married ever since.

Now that I look back, I know how lucky I am to have Stacey as my wife. I know that she was the perfect girl God has chosen for me. Even though my high school girlfriend was really nice, loved my family and wrestling, she wasn't the perfect one for me. Don Rohn was the perfect man for her. When I speak at wrestling camps, I tell everyone that the girl from Clarion made a wise choice. Instead of sticking with a knucklehead like me, she chose one of the greatest coaches in history. Don was the head coach of Northampton High School for many years. His teams were state and National Champs many times. Don has coached many great college wrestlers. He also says that much of his success is because of his wife.

God has the perfect mate waiting just for you, too. You must have patience and faith in what He has planned for you. If you can do that, God will reward you with all the things you have ever desired.

Mom

"No man is poor who has had a godly mother."
Abraham Lincoln

The best way to describe my mom is by saying she was an angel sent from God. I know, I know—I've said it before but she truly was. She took on the role of coach's wife, fundraiser, family bus driver and the best cheerleader I ever had. The Gov was the hard driving, tough to please, disciplinarian that coached and demanded perfection. When I didn't reach the high expectations it was Mom who put her arm around me, telling me she still loved me. She would keep secrets away from my Dad when she knew something would disappoint him. For every operation I had, Mom was always right by my bedside. She made each of us six kids feel like we were her favorite. She was the perfect mother-in-law to my wife, Stacey. When we became pregnant for the first time, Stacey couldn't wait to call Mom with the great news. She knew that Mom would react in a way that would make everyone happy. The sad thing about Mom was that she was a smoker.

She didn't know the cigarette companies put things in the cigarettes to make it almost impossible to quit. Mom smoked for over 40 years to the displeasure of her family. She finally did quit smoking and was so proud to call us and share the good news. But, it was too late. Three years later she was diagnosed with lung cancer. I watched my mother battle cancer for the last 15 months of her life. Losing my mom was one of the biggest tests of faith I have had to go through. I miss her greatly! My dad, however, had the hardest time during Mom's fight against cancer. He was mad at the doctors, especially when they told us that Mom had put up a good fight but there wasn't anything else they could do. Dad thought there might be an experimental drug that we could try. His "never give up attitude" didn't mesh with the seemingly hopeless diagnosis for his wife of 48 years and her battle with cancer.

My dad was also mad at God.

"Why would a loving God take away an angel like your mom," he would ask.

Nobody ever prepares you for the death and funeral of your mother. Carrying Mom's casket into the old church that she grew up in was very hard to do. My five brothers and sisters were all helping carry the casket, crying their hearts out. I felt it was the time for me, the Christian, to be the strong pillar of our family. Speaking at a funeral is not the most popular thing to do. As a Christian, you have an open line of communication with the Lord. God told me that I should be the one representing my family by giving the eulogy. I asked God to give me the strength to tell everyone at that church what a blessed woman my mom was. God answered my prayers again.

Adversity is part of the process that God uses to produce good results in our lives. Trouble, if turned to the Lord, could actually be the best for our lives. You **will** face adversity, but having a blessed life will help you get through it.

Having a blessed life means you will truly have a "new" best friend. When you think about some of the friends in your life, you realize it was because of the amount of time you spent with them. You can also spend time with Jesus through prayer. Prayer is an open line, straight to heaven. Just like a best friend, you don't have to be afraid to tell God what you are thinking. I call Jesus your best friend because He is always listening. When I can't go back to sleep at night, I know it is God wanting to speak to me, without any distractions. He hears every little thing I say and will tell me the things I need to do. I find myself talking to Him when things are bothering me. I think of mean things to say to a person I am having problems with at work and God will catch me and say, "Don't talk, just pray." I know that all good gifts come from God, so I give credit where credit is due. Before closing my eyes at night, I think back on the day, thanking God for getting me through it.

Ryan Tate

Jesus never pointed out the weaknesses of people, never dwelt on the failures and their shortcomings. He simply said, "Go and sin no more. Be what God intends you to be."

I have been lucky enough to coach a state champion

and another wrestler who was a high school All-American. Joe Tezak was an NAIA national champ for the University of Mary. But they were not the greatest wrestlers I've ever coached. The best wrestler I ever had took fifth in the state, as a junior. His name is Ryan Tate.

I can remember when my friend, Joe Ismay, told me that he had a really good wrestler from Oklahoma at his middle school. The boy was going to come to Mount Carmel High School and he had the most supportive dad ever.

Ryan had all the qualities of a champion wrestler. He was quick and fast. He had an explosive double leg takedown. He was mean and would slam you on your head if he could. Most of all, he was competitive. When our team would go for long runs, I would try to get kids to hold Ryan back as I would sprint to the finish line. I would be trying my hardest, not to let him catch me. Most of the other wrestlers would give up on the run, especially when I would pass them, but not Ryan. Right before I crossed the finish line, Ryan would fly by me. That competitive nature is hard to teach. I knew that I had a stud.

During his junior year, Ryan worked out really hard. We brought in a college wrestler to wrestle with Ryan every day after school. At the end of the year, Ryan was taking him down ten times in a row. Ryan ended up winning our county tournament and placing fifth in the state of California. I thought that we were going to have another state champion, but then, things started changing. When I got to school before Ryan's senior year, kids would come and tell me stories about Ryan. See, I have people I call my "spies." These are kids around school that know I'm a Christian. They have seen the way I live my life, both on and off the wrestling mats. They know what I stand for. They know that I don't want my wrestlers partying, so when they see them doing so, they tell me.

My spies came and told me that Ryan had been going to the parties. Ryan was not leading the type of lifestyle that state champions led. One day, in the fall, I saw Ryan in his football uniform walking out to practice. I pulled Ryan to the side and said, "Ryan, my spies have been telling me you've been partying."

Ryan's head immediately dropped. I asked him, "Ryan. What do you want to accomplish this year as a wrestler?"

He said, "Coach, I want to be a state champion."

I said, "Ryan, there's no way that God is going to let you be a state champion if you're a partier. You need to stop and think about what you really want to accomplish as a senior."

Ryan shook his head and said, "I know, Coach."

I guess my speech wasn't that good, because Ryan continued his bad lifestyle. He was one of the leading tacklers on our football team, but hurt his shoulder during the season. In the first wrestling tournament of the year, Ryan re- injured his shoulder. The doctors told him there was no way that he could wrestle. The only possibility would come from resting his shoulder from December to February, and then maybe have a chance to wrestle in the end of the year tournaments.

I thought that watching his teammates wrestle, knowing how successful he could have been if he was out there, would motivate Ryan to change his lifestyle. One thing didn't change were the people Ryan associated himself with. They weren't really looking out for his best interest and Ryan continued to party. In the semi-finals of our CIF tournament, Ryan looked at me with a grimaced look that said it all, "Hey, coach. My shoulder's hurt and I can't go on."

Ryan's Dad was not only the most supportive dad that I ever encountered, he was also very pro-active. He made a highlight tape of Ryan during his junior and senior year and sent it out to colleges around the country. This brought a lot of interest and Bill Lamb of the University of North Carolina gave Ryan a wrestling scholarship. Ryan's Dad set up a scholarship signing party and brought in all of Ryan's coaches including Coach Lamb, who flew out from North Carolina.

I tried to tell Ryan that God was giving him a second

chance. North Carolina "never gives scholarships to California kids; so take advantage of it."

He said, "I know, Coach. I'm not going to blow it this time."

That fall, Ryan called me up from North Carolina and said, "Coach, you won't believe the workout partners I have. Kendall Cross, Olympic champion, is my assistant coach. The other assistant is T. J. Jaworsky, three-time NCAA champion." He said, "The facilities at North Carolina are beautiful." At Thanksgiving break, Ryan flew home and brought me North Carolina wrestling sweatshirts and nice shoes all in Carolina blue. Ryan was so successful that he made the starting lineup at 142-pounds. This in itself is a remarkable feat, to crack the lineup as a true freshman.

Ryan came home for Christmas vacation, telling me that he had to work out for the Midland's tournament. He had to get his weight down and wanted to attend our high school practices. I knew something was up when Ryan didn't show up once. Of course, when he flew to the Midland's tournament, Ryan didn't make weight. Making weight in wrestling is a commitment thing. When you say you are going to do something, the team is counting on you. College coaches are paying for your education and making weight is part of your job description.

Coach Lamb yelled at Ryan right in front of his mom. Instead of being remorseful, Ryan reverted back to his bad life-style choices. Later in the month, I get a phone call from the University of Oklahoma's wrestling coach, Jack Spates. I grew up with Jack, and he told me how excited he was that Ryan was going to transfer to OU.

Ryan knew of the mistakes he had made. The move to Oklahoma was a new start for Ryan. He began his new life by recommitting himself to Christ. Instead of trying to please his parents or his old high school coach, Ryan decided that pleasing God was his number one priority. The fear of failing Christ was his motivational drive that has stuck with him from that moment until today. He changed his life around and was back in the state he grew up in. Ryan stopped partying and became a member of the Oklahoma University Wrestling Team. Even though he wasn't able to make the starting line-up, Ryan was a very important part of their team that won the conference championship. Now, Ryan has a beautiful wife and daughter (most wrestlers have daughters–go figure), graduated from the University of Oklahoma and is President of one of the leading publishers of Christian books in the country.

The future is bright if Christ is your hope. Our earthly lives will have a greater significance. Through constant prayers, our behavior and Christian witness, we become **partners** with God. This is another example of how the lessons you teach may take about eight to ten years to take effect. Ryan's life is a perfect example how God rewards people who work extremely hard and lead good lifestyles.

Involvement in FCA

Reach out and touch as many people as you can. Your impact on these young people can be significant

When I got my teaching job at Mount Carmel, I noticed the basketball coach had a plaque on his wall. The Fellowship of Christian Athletes honored our coach for his involvement in the organization.

One day, the coach gave me a copy of *Victory Magazine,* the monthly publication of FCA. In the magazine was an article about a high school wrestling coach from the Los Angeles area. This coach would have Bible studies with his wrestlers and take them to the FCA Summer Camp.

The very next weekend, I was at a wrestling tournament. I'm sitting in the stands and right next to me is the coach who was in the article. I said, "Hey! Aren't you the guy they wrote the article about in the *FCA Magazine?*"

Scott Glabb smiled and said, "Boy! I didn't think anyone ever read that magazine."

Since I had been involved with wrestling camps my whole life, I asked Scott if there was any way I could help out at the camp. He sat and spoke about FCA and all of the great things the organization did for high school athletes.

This was another example of God working in my life. Scott has been a very close friend of mine ever since that day. He raises money each year to send over 30 of his Santa Ana High School wrestlers to FCA camps. The relationship between Scott's wrestlers and me is something I cherish. The Santa Ana boys do not have many material things, but what they do have is a competitive spirit that sets them apart. We share a Hispanic background and I consider those wrestlers as my second team I coach. At FCA summer camps, I get a chance to meet other Christian coaches and hear how they get through their sport; balancing their faith with the sport and coaching. It has been a blessing for my family to get away and share how the Lord has changed my life. Taking a page from the story Pastor Sean shared at Horizon, our kids at camp call themselves, "Wrestlers for Christ." We make t-shirts for all of the wrestlers and ask them to wear them whenever they make the finals of a tournament as a visual testimony of their faith.

I've been able to share my testimony at different FCA functions. FCA in San Diego has a great organization with Donnie Dee leading it. There was no leadership at all in Fellowship of Christian Athletes when I came to San Diego. Jim Garner, the regional director, was able to bring Donnie from Colorado to be the Southern California director. Now, I believe we have over 55 schools that have FCA huddles. Kids meet at lunchtime and have professional athletes or youth pastors share their testimony on how Jesus has changed their lives. Stacey and I love the Fellowship of Christian Athletes and plan to be apart of the organization for the rest of our lives.

Johnny Jones

Those who trust in God find comfort in His power.

Johnny Jones was a wrestler for Iowa State University, during the same time my friend, Bobby Antonacci was there. They were good friends and became Christians together. Johnny wrestled at 118-pounds for Iowa State and that year the NCAA Tournament was in Ames, Iowa, the home of Iowa State. Most of the participating college teams arrive two days before the NCAA tournament begins. On Wednesday, the day before the tournament, all the teams are there working hard, trying to get their weight down. They practice in the arena, which usually holds eight wrestling mats. This allows enough room for most of the college wrestlers to work out at the same time.

Johnny had this special move that helped him become very successful. During the workout on Wednesday wanting to get everyone's attention, Johnny yelled, "Hey! Listen, everybody! I want to show you my favorite move. This move has been very successful for me and maybe it can help you. I just want to show it to you." He said, "I learned this move in a dream."

Since Johnny was a Christian, he told everyone that God showed him this move in his dream so he called the move "Jesus". He actually used the Spanish pronunciation for the word, Jesus. Wrestlers and coaches stared in awe because this was of unheard of . . . the day before the biggest tournament of the year, a wrestler named Johnny Jones would be giving away his secret move to everybody—even his opponents. Johnny, you see, trusted in God and the talent that God had given him to work hard and to lead a good lifestyle. He was not afraid because his faith was his power, his might and ultimately his glory.

Johnny proceeded to get on the mat and demonstrate the technique for all to see. He told them how easy it was to score points and "maybe the move can help you, too." Johnny went on to make it all the way to the NCAA finals and become an

All-American. Ever since I learned of that story, our high school team uses that move only now we call it "The Johnny Jones".

A little side note to that story: Johnny's younger brother is named Zeke Jones. Zeke was our 2004 Olympic coach in Athens and is one of the top college wrestling coaches in the country.

Chapter Eleven

CLOSING WORDS

After finishing my 28th year of coaching, I decided to step down as head coach and move into the role of assistant. This change has provided me an opportunity to reflect back and evaluate the road my life has traveled. My coaching career started as an assistant and now I have come full circle. After having the total responsibility of a head coach for 20 years, becoming an assistant coach is very exciting. I must tell you this past year has been extremely enjoyable. The competitive fire still burns within me, but now I can sleep better at night.

. I am happy to say that the Gov is still alive and coaching. Wherever he lives, he will find a wrestling program—one he can help and encourage Even though all my brothers and myself are grown men with jobs, families of our own and responsibilities, we don't forget our roots. Every year, it is top priority that in the spring we all meet at the NCAA tournament to watch three days of great wrestling and to spend time with our dad, the Gov. A man who was difficult and demanding to live with, but now as a father with children of my own, I have a better perspective and appreciation for his style. Today, he has learned how to express how proud he is of me as well as show his love.

My last year as a head coach, the drive to win the championship became my *god*. Instead of wanting "God's will", I thought I knew what was best for me. Having been in second place my whole life, whether I was competing or coaching, led me to feel it was time for a change. I had convinced myself that winning the championship would bring me the personal recognition that I felt was important. Other coaches at my high school, Mt Carmel, had championship banners hanging in the gym. In my observation, they had not put in half the amount of time I did. Technique and strategy, class and close knit family—these were the pillars of my coaching style. In *my* book, I DESERVED to win. However, God saw things differently.

When wrestling season came around year after year, I would change into a totally different person. I was always in a bad mood, never smiling. Opposing coaches would see my facial expressions at tournaments and say, "Come on, things aren't that bad!" Each year after the season, I would reflect, especially on graduation day. When I first became a coach, the Gov made me promise to always attend my school's graduation ceremony. He felt it was the opportunity to support the young men who had given four years of their life to you, their coach. Therefore, every year you will see me at the graduation and you can easily pick me out of the crowd. I am the one in the back row crying as each of my senior wrestlers walk by and hug me. As each boy walks by, I feel as if one of my sons were leaving home. The Holy Spirit asks me, "What kind of impact did you have on that boy? Did your words build him up or knock him down? When these kids look at you, do they see a coach who wanted to win or do they see the love of Christ? Do they want to be like you or are they happy to be moving on?"

God makes you evaluate yourself. I asked Him to change me and again He has answered my prayers. As previously stated, I believed that a wise man learns from his mistakes. I have learned that positive and encouraging people are much more fun to be around. The wrestling shorts our team wears during practice have the word "faith" written across the back. How could I expect my wrestlers to have faith, when I, the leader, did not demonstrate it?

This year, I decided to be that positive, encouraging person God made me to be. Instead of worrying about the welfare of 70 wrestlers, I concentrated on those who needed God's love. Walking around the practice room, I could see who needed my attention. Whether it was technical help or just a hug of encouragement, God was showing me the new chapter of my life. Not only could I affect the wrestlers, but the new head coach needed a mentor. Just as Christians need an accountability partner, young coaches also need an accountability or mentor figure.

With the change in my coaching role, my priorities have changed and so have our team's results. I am happy to say that a banner will finally hang in the gym with the word "Wrestling" on it. Other coaches have asked, "Aren't you sad that the year you step down is the year you finally win?" My response is, NO. Society wants gold medals and championship banners, but God wants a pure heart. He knows the true intent behind all the things you do. I now have security of heart, knowing I am doing God's will.

I have a wife and two daughters that need me to be a better husband and dad. Before I was a coach who had a family and now I am a dad who also coaches. It is like being a coach who is a Christian compared to a Christian coach. Why do you thing God has you competing or coaching? To win championships, or to bring people closer to the Lord?

Where To Go From Here?

Having turned 50 in 2005, I see myself heading into a different direction. Up until now, I have felt my purpose in life was to prepare young men for life after high school using the platform of wrestling. I know that God gives all of us different talents. Teaching wrestling has always been one of those God-given talents for me. But He has also blessed me with the ability to motivate through communication and telling stories. My pastor told me that the time from 50 to 70 years of age, are the most productive years. My goals are now to get closer to God and use my speaking ability to get others closer to God.

Instead of focusing only on high school athletes, I feel

the need and desire to help coaches. FCA has a Coaches & their Wives (or Husbands) Get-Away weekend. An opportunity to stay in a really nice hotel, learn from motivational speakers and to share stories with other coaches. My wife and I want to encourage and financially support all Christian coaches to attend something similar.

Being a mentor to other coaches starts with my walking closely with God and being the role model he has designed me to be. The lack of value in the marriage vows is ruining our society and I see the impact everyday in my classroom. God brought to me the perfect woman with whom to spend my life. He has also given me the responsibility to be the husband she can rely upon especially during tough times. God has also blessed me with two daughters, which is a very scary thing. I watch freshman girls fall for all the tricks older boys present. I see them craving the attention but not looking at the consequences. This enforces the importance of my own children being grounded in the Lord. I want to be a supportive father and husband and the only way is with my eyes on the Lord.

When I look back on this year and the decision I made to step down as head coach, I remember how I cried when I told my team of the decision. Being a head coach was the dream I had had since I was 7 years old, but God was talking to me. I remember being sad and depressed and turned my eyes and heart to heaven and that is when God changed the desires of my heart. God was giving me a different purpose. This new purpose has not always been clear, it is being revealed day by day. My new purpose began when God had me visit one of my ex-wrestlers who is now a book publisher. I have a new goal to work towards and I am very excited.

To The Athletes:

I wrote this book so you could learn from my mistakes, and with the hope that you will realize you are not alone and it is not too late. Whenever I look at an old wrestling picture of myself, I stand out! I am the one with my head down, getting the second place medal. The champion is all smiles as he looks down on me. I want to encourage you to "LOOK UP"! You can be in that first place spot. You are the son or daughter of the most powerful God. When you give your life to Jesus, He takes over as your real head coach. You can overcome your mistakes and shortcomings through the belief in God. There is limitless power to those who believe, but first you must believe. God did not make you to settle for second place. There is incredible power inside you when you believe in God's plan for your life. It is not how you feel but what you believe and many times we let our feelings drive our actions. There is only one thing that keeps you from winning—you and the decisions you make. Focus on God, listen to God and act for God—do not be afraid.

Even though I may not know you, I am concerned about your struggles. Whether it is on the field, or the mat, or off, I would love to hear from you. Maybe you can't talk with your parents or you are not that close to your coach. Please know I am just an email away. I promise to get back with you. I can be reached at José_campo@hotmail.com.

Recall what I have tried to say in this book, *Wisdom From the Corner.* Remember that by working extremely hard and leading a good lifestyle, God will reward you. You have the power to live in victory. Our Team Wins!

FORTY WRESTLERS
FOR CHRIST

Nero was a Roman Emperor who surrounded himself with personal bodyguards. These bodyguards were the strongest, bravest and best athletes chosen from the Roman Amphitheater. Of course, they were wrestlers. Instead of worshipping Nero, these wrestlers were Christians. News reached Nero that many of his Roman soldiers had accepted the Christian faith. Nero sent a decree to Vespasian, the leader of these guards stating, "If any soldier clings to the Christian faith, they must die!" The decree was received in the winter while the wrestlers were camped on the shore of a frozen lake. Vespasian called the wrestlers together and asked, "Are there any among you who cling to the Christian faith?"

All forty wrestlers, without hesitation, stepped forward and stood at attention. Vespasian pleaded with them to save their lives by denying this Christian faith, but not a single one denied the Lord. Finally he ordered them to strip down and march to the center of the frozen lake. As they marched, the wrestlers chanted,

> "Forty wrestlers for Thee, Oh, Christ,
> to win for Thee the victory
> and from Thee the victor's crown."

Throughout the night, Vespasian sat by the fire and watched. As the night went on, the chant grew fainter. As morning came, one wrestler crawled back to the fire, denouncing the Lord. From the distance, Vespasian heard the chant,

"Thirty-nine wrestlers for Christ. . . ."

Overwhelmed by the remaining wrestlers' loyalty, and convicted of his own sins and need for a Savior, Vespasian took off his helmet and clothes and walked to the lake's center, replacing the one who recanted. He held his head high as he joined the chant,

"Forty wrestlers for Thee, Oh, Christ. . . ."

As the morning dawned, forty frozen bodies lay upon the icy surface.

Be a wrestler for Christ. Our team wins!
I would like to hear FROM YOU!
Even though I may not know you, I do care about you. If you are an athlete, coach or parent and this book has touched you, I would enjoy hearing from you.

jose_campo@hotmail.com

Contact author José Campo
or order more copies of this book at

TATE PUBLISHING, LLC

127 East Trade Center Terrace
Mustang, Oklahoma 73064

(888) 361 - 9473

Tate Publishing, LLC

www.tatepublishing.com